T0118179

Lady Grayl

Naturalist, ornithologist, educator and poet, Dr. Robert Nero's acclaimed "Great Gray Owl: Phantom of the Northern Forest" was the first of the Smithsonian Institution's Nature Books. It was followed by their "Redwings", also by Nero, thus bringing to a wide audience spirited accounts of his involvement with those two species. Recent publication of two collections of poetry: "Woman By the Shore" and "The Mulch Pile", by Natural Heritage, reveals his wide grasp of environmental matters and human nature.

"Lady Grayl – Owl With A Mission" is a true account of Nero's close relationship with a tame Great Gray Owl. His keen perception of this bird's behaviour, and those of her kind, coupled with sensitive writing, provides charming insights to bird and man alike. This is the story of their journey together, their joint mission, a remarkable account that will stand long after they are gone.

This is more than a book about an owl and its presumed mission, this is a book as well about a gifted person who has helped usher in a new era of understanding and appreciation of birds of prey. It is the educational aspect of Dr. Nero's endeavours that impresses us most. Now seventy-one years old, he continues to help schoolchildren and their mentors better appreciate the complexity and beauty of wildlife.

Lady Grayl

Owl With A Mission

by Robert W. Nero

Natural Heritage/Natural History Inc.

Lady Grayl: owl with a mission
By Robert W. Nero
Published by Natural Heritage/Natural History Inc.
P.O. Box 95, Station O
Toronto, Ontario M4A 2M8
© 1994 Robert W. Nero
All Rights Reserved

No portion of this book, with the exception of brief extracts for the purpose of literary review, may be reproduced in any form without the permission of the publishers.

Design: Derek Chung Tiam Fook
Printed and bound in Canada by Hignell Printing Limited
Winnipeg, Manitoba

Canadian Cataloguing in Publication Data

Nero, Robert W., 1922-
    Lady Grayl: owl with a mission

Includes bibliographical references and index.
ISBN: 978-0-920474-94-5

1. Lady Grayl (Owl). 2. Great gray owl.
I. Title.

QL696.S83N4 1994   598.9'7   C94-932441-8

Natural Heritage/Natural History Inc. gratefully acknowledges the assistance of the Canada Council, the Ontario Arts Council, and the Government of Ontario through the Ministry of Culture, Tourism & Recreation.

Cover Photo:
Lady Grayl and author, May 16, 1992, Lower Nelson River, Gillam, Manitoba

Back Cover Photo:
Lady Grayl with the Balmoral Hall girls.

Dedication

This book has to be dedicated to my wife, Ruth F. Nero.
Only family members and close friends know how supportive
she has been over the course of nearly half a century.
Without her, it is unlikely that my involvement with
a tame owl could or would have happened.

Thank you, Ruth.

Table of Contents

Teacher

It takes a tame owl
to show me things
I'd otherwise miss
or overlook
or lose the importance of
such as
dead, dry aspen leaves
still on their twigs
rustling in a cold breeze
set to tapping against
each other -
a small thing
but it caught the owl's
attention for a moment
her head tipped up
motionless, watchful, listening
a delicate fall sound
I'd heard before
but never perceived.

From Woman by the Shore, and Other Poems, by R.W. Nero,
published by Natural Heritage/Natural History Inc. Toronto, 1990

Preface

TWO BIRDS, THE RED-WINGED BLACKBIRD AND THE GREAT GRAY OWL, have considerably affected my life. For six years, 1948 to 1953, during my university studies at Madison, Wisconsin, I watched and recorded the behaviour of redwings. Their social interactions and displays fascinated me; by immersing myself in their lives, I grew and developed as an ornithologist. Eventually, my observations provided the basis for a Ph.D. thesis. It may seem a long way from blackbirds to owls, from cattail marshes to boreal forest bogs, but it all happened as naturally as growing old. My sojourn with the great gray owl (*Strix nebulosa*), which began in 1968, has now covered twenty-five years, and the end is not in sight.

I have written and lectured at length about great gray owls, and have been involved with five graduate students who have done research on this species, namely: Maureen L. Bouchart, K. Michael Collins, James R. Duncan, Steven L. Loch and Maria C. Servos. Our success in this venture may be judged by their theses. Results of an extensive telemetry study of the great gray owl, in which more than 100 owls were radio-marked, will appear in a monograph by Jim Duncan. Jim's Ph.D. thesis describes some fascinating aspects of great gray owl ecology, including relationships between owls and voles. Strategies for survival in low vole years send owls northward as far as the Hudson Bay Lowlands. So electronic gadgetry has helped shed light on the world of the great gray owl, without diminishing our admiration for the beauty and wonder of this bird.

For the past several years, I've functioned primarily as a fund-raiser to help support great gray owl research and the Manitoba peregrine falcon and burrowing owl recovery projects. I have also provided funding for the Manitoba Wildlife Rehabilitation Organization and the Manitoba Conservation Data Centre. Since these fund-raising efforts have incorporated an educational aspect, the benefits have been twofold. A tame great gray owl, a bird taken from a nest and reared for purposes of education, research and fund-raising, has provided an important impetus to these endeavours. The publicity attached to our activities with this bird has also played a major role in obtaining research funding from numerous sources, including World Wildlife Fund Canada, Abitibi-Price Inc., and The Murphy Foundation.

In my earlier book, Phantom of the Northern Forest, I closed with these words: "In my own pursuit of the owl, I crave further understanding... But ah! if we could perceive the world of the owl, what strange sounds and beautiful forms we might enjoy!" That's probably a vain thought, but I like to think that in small ways this tame owl is providing insights into the nature of that world. This book is about this bird.

Originally called simply "Gray'l" or "Grayl," the name "Lady Grayl" was recently bestowed upon this bird as a kind of formal designation to dignify this now well-known celebrity. The name also identifies the gender, which is almost the first thing people want to know about her.

Incidentally, there are two ways of spelling the colour gray/grey. Canadians tend to spell it grey, following the British tradition, but in the U.S. it's generally gray. For names of birds, however, there is a rule. In North America, the official standard spelling for bird names is the American Ornithologists' Union Checklist, in which it is great gray owl. In England and Europe, the standard English spelling is set by the British Ornithologists' Union, using, of course, great grey owl. I've always insisted that it be spelled gray, so it's been a source of annoyance to me to find so many friends and associates in the U.S. using the British spelling! Well, it's the same bird, whatever way its name is spelled.

"Lady Grayl" has now been out in public on more than 250 occasions. At one time or another, Grayl has been the featured performer at press conferences, TV and radio interviews, government functions, museums, lecture halls, banquets, clubs, shopping malls, trade shows, sportsmen's shows and nursing homes, but schools (university, collegiate and elementary) are her forte. This one great gray owl has offered many thousands of people an opportunity to experience the grandeur and regal nature of the creature that Swedish ornithologist Ove Steffanson unequivocally calls: "The most beautiful bird in the world!" I find it hard to disagree with that sentiment, exaggerated though it may be. I've watched wild great gray owls under a variety of circumstances, have handled several hundred for banding, and for the past several years have lived in close association with a tame one. It is a privilege to have access to a great gray owl that I can observe at close range day and night. It is an experience that I have tried to share with others.

At the age of seventy-one, I still find myself involved in a school tour program, taking Lady Grayl to elementary schools. It gives youngsters, teachers and parents an opportunity to enjoy the bird, and for me to pass along some of the pleasure and interest I've found in working with her. Is this a suitable role for the Manitoba government's volunteer "Senior Ecologist"? Is it worthwhile? Apart from a sense of obligation to do this, because that's partly why we took her from the wild, I am motivated by the pleasure and excitement that underlies a school tour. But there is something more. To help get students to study birds of prey, not just to worry about fractions and adverbs, but to embrace the world of the owl as well, that is what is behind all this business of taking an owl to school.

When I look back over my life and try to identify things or situations that encouraged my interest in birds, one that stands out in my memory is sitting and looking at a mounted barn owl on top of a bookcase. This happened when I was eight or nine years old. I was living in an orphanage and was being punished for some silly thing I'd done or not done, and was forced to sit by myself in a seldom-used parlour. So I had time to look at the barn owl, lots of times. I like to compare that incident with now, when youngsters get to see this live, tame owl. Who knows how the experience of meeting this bird may affect them?

Grayl is not the first owl to have been used as an educational bird, but I doubt that any other owl has met so many people and had so much influence. "Owls as Educators" is the title of a chapter in a recent book, The Enchanting Owl, by Connie Toops. At many of the five hundred raptor rehabilitation centres in the U.S. and Canada, non-releasable hawks and owls are used in public displays to foster an interest in raptor conservation. Toops points out that some birds, having the right temperament and trust, function well as educators. Raptors kept for educational purposes in the U.S. are held under long-term educational permits issued by the U.S. Fish and Wildlife Service. In Canada, each province and territory has jurisdiction over raptors, permits being provided by appropriate local authorities. Lady Grayl is kept by me under the auspices of the Manitoba Department of Natural Resources.

Being well adjusted to people, Grayl readily accepts our company without fear, aggression or stress. Thus, she provides a marvellous opportunity for a wide audience to see a bird of prey at close hand, to admire and appreciate its beauty, and to develop an improved perception of the role of raptors. Grayl is an appropriate ambassador for her kind. Those birds in the remote woodlands, no less beautiful and interesting, are the ones for which we have the most concern.

It has been my good fortune for the past nine years to visit with this owl almost daily, to travel with her over thousands of kilometres, to take her to a variety of places and to bask in her glory. Grayl also has been my inspiration for three poems published in Woman by the Shore and three in The Mulch Pile. I have included these poems and one other about her here. We will never know how many persons have been touched by the grace of this one particular bird, but it pleases me to think that a lot of people have fond memories of her beauty, have been moved by her pleasant nature, have had their lives enriched by this owl with a mission.

The late Louise de Kiriline Lawrence, reflecting on the various activities in which we've been involved over the years, wrote to tell me that through our work we were "helping to fulfil the destiny of the great gray owl." I like to think that in the same way, the great gray owl is helping us to fulfil our own destinies.

Acknowledgements

HERBERT W. R. COPLAND AND I HAVE WORKED CLOSELY TOGETHER over many years in the field, constructing nest-platforms to attract great gray owls. The success of this venture has been the primary basis for the research on this species. The owl featured in this book came from one of the nests that Herb and I built. Herb's constant good humour, tolerance and interest in the project for so long a period are much appreciated.

I am particularly indebted to Renate Scriven. Without her interest, enthusiasm and experience in rehabilitating wild birds, we would never have taken an owl from the wild. Nor would it have been possible to raise this owl without the support of the entire Scriven family.

Katherine McKeever, C.M., LL.D., founder of the Owl

*Herbert W. R. Copland and author with newly-captured
great gray owl, Lac du Bonnet, Manitoba.*

Rehabilitation Research Foundation, provided wise counsel and advice during the early period of our involvement with Lady Grayl. I expect no less any time I need to phone Kay. Brian Ratcliff designed two homes for our owl, and supervised the construction of the present one. He also gave much moral support to the project.

For making available a constant supply of owl food in the form of dead mice and rats, I am deeply grateful to the University of Manitoba Health Sciences (campus and downtown) and Animal Sciences departments. Several students and workers associated with those breeding facilities routinely bagged and froze carcasses for us, namely: Shah Amal, Randy Babiuk, Paul Boehm, Shirley Bond, Sophie Bouchard, Gillia Davis, Alice Dennis, Terry Garner, Corinna Jasienczyk, Terry Lees, Robert Migliore and Ron Taylor.

Thanks to art dealer Ed Purvis, and artist Terry McLean, we were able to sell great gray owl limited edition plates at a considerable profit. Robert R. Taylor contributed photos of Grayl for a button and a colour print; both are still popular items.

Many volunteers have helped me present the owl to the public at one time or another. Special thanks are owing to Linda Anderson, Ron Black, Maureen Bouchart, Sophie Bouchard, Andria Cole, Herb and Beverly Copland, Hazel Dykes, Connie Dzus and family, Jim and Patsy Duncan, Cheryl Graham, Merv Haines and family, Lisa Handford, Karen and Darryl Johnson, Sandra Konrad, Lisa Love, Rhonda O'Grady, Ilme Liepins, Heather Purvis, Ulrike Schneider, Al Schritt, Jack and Jean Scriven, Renate Scriven, Marianne and Max Setliff, Robert R. Taylor and Doug Wareham.

Thanks for various services are also due the following: Dianna Sahulka, Yvonne Jansen, Theresa Campanelli and Geoff Plouffe.

For assistance in organizing extended school tour itineraries, in arranging for accommodation and other services, and for hospitality, I am indebted to the regional staff of the Department of Natural Resources, particularly Craig

Asselstine, Dennis Ayotte, A. Lane Boles, Cam Elliott, George Granberg, Ken Horn, Joe Johannesson, Sid Robak, Dave Roberts, and Pierce Roberts. Several school teachers provided assistance in this same connection, especially Bill Walley, Carole Anderson, Jodi Stepaniuk and Olga Wesner.

Corinna Jasienczyk assisted me with numerous presentations at malls, government functions, schools, etc., first as a volunteer over a two-year period, then as a casual employee of the Wildlife Branch during the 1991 season. Her sound advice helped improve the owl school tour program in many ways. Corinna also typed an initial portion of the manuscript.

For constant support and encouragement, I am grateful to my former supervisor, Dr. Merlin W. Shoesmith, now Assistant Deputy Minister, Department of Natural Resources. Merlin tolerated a lot of misdirected abuse from me, but his confidence in me never wavered. Richard C. Goulden, formerly Director of the Wildlife Branch and Assistant Deputy Minister, Natural Resources, was strongly supportive throughout my years with the Wildlife Branch. The Honourable Harry Enns, Minister, Natural Resources, was also supportive, as were previous Ministers. Thanks also are due to colleagues in Fisheries and Wildlife who accepted my often anxious state with forbearance.

The Department of Natural Resources has provided considerable financial support for our activities. For a year after I retired in May 1991, I worked for the Department under contract. Since then, grants from the Department's Special Conservation Fund and the Winnipeg-based Murphy Foundation have enabled me to continue the owl school tour program.

For encouragement in writing this book, and for assistance in typing the manuscript, I could hardly hope for a more willing and pleasant colleague, companion and friend than Betty Struthers. She typed and typed, and retyped, and provided inspiration, and tea, and a sense of direction when I needed it. Thanks, Betty. Robert P. Berger, Rosemarie Young and Judy Grandmont also helped in the physical production of the manuscript.

James R. Duncan, Yvonne Jansen, Ted Muir, Carol A. Scott and Merlin W. Shoesmith kindly reviewed all or part of the manuscript at one stage or another. I am grateful for their comments.

I am especially grateful to all those persons whose photographs appear in this book; their names, where known, are given. Jim Tallosi kindly provided useful guidance in sorting through numerous photographs. Brendan Carruthers helped greatly with arrangement of photographs and text, and other matters.

My thanks to my dear wife, Ruth, necessarily end this section. Almost daily for the past seven years, this dependable woman has had to remember to take mice out of her freezer to thaw on the kitchen counter, so that when I come home they are ready to take out to the owl. It's not many times that she has forgotten. Ruth's patient acceptance of my moodiness and her calm, loving concern for my well-being have made it possible for me to persist in these endeavours.

CHAPTER 1

Taken from the Wild

HIKING THROUGH DEEP WET SNOW IN APRIL 1968, 16 KM NORTH OF The Pas, Manitoba, both of us carrying equipment to build a photography tower at an active great gray owl nest, punster Robert R. Taylor stopped to say: "Well, Nero, we can always think of this as the search for the Holy 'Gray'l'." Sixteen years later, I named a young gray owl "Gray'l" (for convenience, hereafter, spelled "Grayl"). That bird, taken as a chick from a nest in southeastern Manitoba for educational purposes, and now more than ten years old, is the subject of this book.

The Pas nest, found by local resident Phil Reader, was only the third one known in Manitoba. That trip was the first time either Taylor or I had seen this rare species; it was also the beginning of a close and continuing involvement with great gray owls. In the fall of 1968, large numbers of great gray owls unexpectedly appeared southeast of Winnipeg, some within an hour's drive from the city. Birders and photographers revelled in their presence and my colleagues and I captured a few for banding. A few years later we discovered that they were nesting in the same area; the owls we had driven 600 km north to The Pas to see were living at our doorstep! Our many experiences with these owls over twelve years have been described in my book, The Great Gray Owl, Phantom of the Northern Forest, illustrated with photos by Taylor, and published in 1980 by the Smithsonian Institution Press.

Right from the beginning, an effort was made to share our admiration for this species with the general public.

Posters, articles in newspapers and magazines, radio and TV interviews, and slide-talks were inspired by time spent in the field with wild great gray owls. Photos taken by Taylor and other photographers allowed me to show what I was talking and writing about. My role in the Manitoba Wildlife Branch as a writer and wildlife specialist gave me opportunity to carry out these activities, my supervisors all being supportive, but much of this was done on my own time and at my expense.

Movie footage taken in 1970 at a great gray owl nest by Dalton Muir and Robert Taylor gave me new material which I offered to audiences across the country; made into a Profiles of Nature video in 1984 by Keg Productions, the film has been shown repeatedly on television here and overseas. A short film made at the same nest by George Cotter added to the repertoire of audio-visual material available to the public. One common aspect of our field work captured on film showed us catching hungry owls by luring them within reach of a net. An artificial mouse cast out and reeled in over the snow with a casting rod brought owls right in to our feet. Footage taken by Neil Rettig appeared on "Ripley's Believe It Or Not" TV program under the title "Fishing For Owls!" and on Lorne Green's "Wilderness World"; we received Green's "Tip-o'-the-hat." Other footage taken by Rettig was used by the BBC.

On a few occasions in those early years there was media coverage of live, and sometimes injured, great gray owls. Three injured owls were brought home and subjected to my inexpert attempts at rehabilitation. Two actually survived and were released. Another badly injured bird brought Kay McKeever out by air from the Owl Rehabilitation Research Foundation in southern Ontario. Kay still has that bird. Still, the possibility of having a tame great gray owl to show to the public had not occurred to me. In retrospect, our eventual use of a tame owl for educational purposes seems a logical outcome of the interest in this rare species. If people hadn't heard about these birds prior to 1984, they were certainly likely to know about them over the next few years.

In 1984, I worked closely with Steven L. Loch, a graduate student at St. Cloud Teacher's College, Minnesota. We began a radio-telemetry study under the auspices of the Manitoba Wildlife Branch to try to determine the lifetime habitat requirements of the great gray owl. That spring, Herb Copland and I intensified our efforts to find active owl nests so that Steve Loch could radio-mark a sample of our breeding population. We had discovered that great gray owls, which don't build nests, could be attracted to man-made platforms. It was a lot easier to erect nest-platforms and check them than to search for owls using hawk nests built in previous years. We were assisted on several days that season by Renate Scriven, then seventeen and already an experienced bird rehabilitator and a raptor enthusiast.

At one man-made nest near Marchand, three chicks had hatched from the four eggs. It soon became apparent that the male was having difficulty finding enough food for his family. All three chicks were begging incessantly; undersized and weak, they clearly weren't getting enough food.

Great gray owls rely heavily on small mammals, especially voles (a kind of short-tailed mouse), for food. If the vole population crashes (declines sharply) after the onset of nesting, the male – the hunter for the family – may not be able to find enough food. Under those circumstances, one or more young may be lost. Unexpected food shortages are not common, but when they do occur, the loss of one or more chicks may increase the chances of survival of the remaining brood. In some cases – and this has also been reported for the short-eared owl – the older chicks may even devour the youngest. When this happens, there's not much one can do about it. Usually, one simply records the event.

On May 21, we found that the youngest owlet in the Marchand nest had two severe cuts on its head, presumably made by its older and larger nest-mates. On our next visit to this nest, we found that conditions had deteriorated. Even before we reached the nest we could hear the chicks begging for food. They were three weeks old, the age when they often begin climbing out onto adjacent branches (hence the term "branching"). However, the youngest was barely able to hold its head up. When Renate suggested that we take the injured chick and let her try to rear it, I hesitated, being reluctant to interfere with nature. Four days later, however, we found conditions even more desperate, and I decided we should try to salvage the chick.

This young great gray owl was taken into captivity for several seasons. Our intention was to rehabilitate the owlet, not for release back to the wild, but for use in education and fundraising in connection with our Wildlife Branch project. Renate and some of her fellow wild bird rehabilitators had taken birds into school classrooms, and it occurred to me that this could be a worthwhile function for an owl that otherwise was almost certain to perish. We recognized that if we were successful, the bird would remain permanently in custody. Removal of this bird from the nest reduced the male owl's workload by about one-third. In the end, the remaining two young were reared

Young Grayl.

successfully and both the young and their parents were radio-marked and monitored. Thus we learned that two months after leaving the nest, Grayl's two siblings were killed and eaten by great horned owls.

The young Grayl, summer 1984.

Nursing It Back to Health

Renate, who held a provincial permit to rehabilitate wildlife, took the owlet into her home to care for it. This involved her parents, Jack and Jean Scriven, and her brother Dwain, for the owl was kept loose for five weeks in the Scriven family room. Cloths carefully draped over furniture provided some safeguard, but a few stains on the couch, chair and rug remained as permanent evidence of the Scriven family's tolerance for the adopted owl. The owl made a rapid adjustment from being in a nest nine metres high in a tamarack and having food presented to it by a female owl, to Renate's skillful care.

That first summer I used mousetraps to obtain food for the owl, setting them in nearby meadows and grassy rights of way. Putting out fifty traps daily in the evening and checking them early the next morning yielded a fair number of meadow voles and a few shrews. As I ran my traplines, I reflected on the time and energy invested by a male owl in providing food for a family. Just as I returned to trap where I learned that voles were more plentiful, so, I reasoned, must an owl learn the hotspots in its hunting territory. Sometime later I discovered an easier source of food: an abundance of dead laboratory mice made available to me on a regular basis from the Animal Science Department of the University of Manitoba. Excess mice, culls, and animals sacrificed at the end of breeding and growth studies were killed with carbon dioxide at my request, and bagged and frozen. Lab mice and rats from the University of Manitoba and Health Sciences Centre remain the sole source of food for this bird, as well as for injured owls and other raptors being treated by volunteer workers of the Manitoba Wildlife Rehabilitation Organization.

The owl gained weight rapidly and her downy plumage soon gave way to full feathers. Long before she could fly, she hopped, ran and jumped about the room. When her flight feathers were partly grown, she was able to make jump-flights

Renate Scriven with Grayl and author

Grayl fully feathered, first winter.

of up to a metre. Before long, Jean Scriven's plants had to be removed from shelves in front of a sunny window. Those shelves became one of Grayl's favourite resting places; from the top shelf she could look over a fence and watch the neighbours. Soon Grayl was flying to the top of an open door; sometimes she rested there on her belly, head hanging down.

Note the feminine pronoun. Initially, we called this bird Grayl, without thinking of the gender. Well, Grayl would have suited either a male or a female, but it wasn't long before we guessed that she was a female. Later, signs of nesting behaviour by Grayl proved that we were right. Once she was fully feathered, it was apparent that the white facial markings, so characteristic of this species, were somewhat reduced in Grayl. The crescent-shaped marks between her eyes, in particular, are less white than in many other birds.

The owl's next move was into a backyard pen. The Department of Natural Resources paid for the gravel floor, but most of the cost came out of Renate's pocket. The whole family was involved in the construction. Oak branches, with their rough bark, made ideal perches, and the pen was large enough so that the owl was able to fly about freely.

For several weeks, to help develop her flying ability, Renate flew Grayl almost daily outside the pen on a 30-metre-long cord fastened to "jesses," small leather anklets on the bird's feet. The jesses are worn all the time. (I have an extra set, and a few times a year switch them around so that I can wash them and rub them with neat's-foot oil to keep them supple.) Right from the start, Grayl seemed able to cope with these necessary encumbrances. Occasionally the jesses get in her way, but generally she handles them well. Many people are not even aware that she's wearing them.

As part of Grayl's training program, she received a mouse when she responded to a whistle and flew 30 m from a perch onto someone's gloved hand. This was fun, and several different people enjoyed this experience. Renate accomplished all this, despite also having looked after numerous injured or orphaned birds that were brought to her over that summer, birds ranging from a hummingbird to a heron, and several hawks and owls.

I participated in flying Grayl and spent a good deal of time sitting with her in her pen. I even spent two nights with her that October, just to see what it would be like, lying in a sleeping bag at the back of the pen. My notes include: "Gave her three mice at 10:00 p.m. when she came to the edge of my bed in response to my whistle...once I whistled and when she came, I didn't give her a mouse, whereupon she stuck her head into my sleeping bag."

A Lesson in Perception

Since we intended to take Grayl in a car to demonstrate at lectures and other events, I began putting her in my compact station wagon for a few hours in evenings in late September. We should have started this when she was younger. By now fully grown, at first she reacted badly to being confined in the car, but by the end of a week she was used to it.

On one of those evening sessions with Grayl, when I was trying to get her used to being in a car, something happened that left a deep impression on me. According to my notes, this was on October 3, 1984. The owl was sitting on her perch in the back of the parked car, looking around calmly. Suddenly, in the house across the street from us, a dog appeared looking out a picture window. It was a white poodle; all that could be seen was its head. With its woolly head and long floppy ears, it had a somewhat owl-like appearance. Grayl instantly reacted to this unexpected apparition, puffing herself up in a remarkable fashion. It was the first time I'd seen a great gray owl give this display. All her plumage was raised as she crouched forward with lowered head; the back feathers, especially, were lifted high, and even the breast feathers were lifted; the wings were partly lowered and the tail was spread. This aggressive-defensive display is found in several, if not all, owl species. At the peak of the display, Grayl gave a hoarse hissing sound, a very antagonistic signal.

This defensive display, making herself look larger than normal, denotes apprehension and deep concern, or so I view it. The display was maintained off and on, rising and falling in intensity, while the owl stared fixedly at the poodle in the window. They watched each other – it appeared that the dog was equally transfixed by the behaviour of the owl – for twenty minutes. Only when the dog left the window did the owl subside. In a few minutes, someone let the poodle outside! I turned to watch the owl, awaiting her reaction. As the poodle slowly trotted up the driveway to the road, the owl gave only a slight display, a mere beginning of her previous performance. Nothing further happened, though she watched the dog steadily for about fifteen minutes. When a little girl came right past the car with a collie on a leash, there was no erection of plumage by the owl. She just watched. After a while, someone let the poodle back in the house. Now for the critical part of

Grayl with author.

this natural experiment! The poodle soon reappeared at the window – the same owl-like face, same place, same way – but this time there was no reaction. Just that fast, the owl appeared to have learned that the peculiar thing in the window was only a dog.

A *Star* Is *Born*

Grayl's first exposure to the general public was at the Fort Whyte Centre for Environmental Education, not a bad place to begin. I stood in their parking lot on an unofficial basis for an hour, holding the bird in hand like a beggar with a cup, to test her reactions. Everyone who passed by was surprised and excited to see an owl up close, and the owl was agreeably relaxed and unafraid. With that experience for assurance, a few days later I took her to Tom Thorsteinson's adult education class at Red River Community College. I talked about great gray owl attributes, the research project, and the need for funding. The students were so impressed that they agreed to hold a fund-raising drive throughout the college. Afterwards, as I headed for my car, owl in hand, I was approached by a lady who asked if her five-year old daughter could please see the bird. I stooped down so that the child could get a good look, but I hadn't counted on the girl rushing forward and hugging the bird; she even kissed it on the bill! I was shocked, but the owl neither flinched nor showed any sign of annoyance. This was my first indication of the tolerance Grayl has for small people. Over the next few days, I made two more visits to the college, and a trip to Centennial school in Selkirk. Renate Scriven and I took turns holding Grayl during a six and one-half hour fund-raising stint at a Selkirk mall. Grayl was on the way to becoming a celebrity.

It was becoming clear that Grayl could handle almost anything. Her capacity for spending long hours amidst noisy crowds and other sights and sounds indicated a remarkable patience and endurance and the extent to which she was imprinted on people. Before long, she would be helping people better appreciate birds of prey by sitting in shopping malls for up to twelve hours a day. Not everyone thought that this was a good idea. A few people objected to subjecting a bird to so much human contact, to taking a bird from the wild, depriving it of its natural life, and keeping it active all day long. I can relate to those concerns. It was partly on that account that I hesitated taking the bird from the nest. But I've never had any regrets. Because she was so well-adjusted to people, she readily accepted being the centre of large crowds, providing a marvellous opportunity for a wide audience to see a bird of prey at close hand.

There are several reasons why this bird can't be turned loose. For one thing, Grayl is afraid of owls or anything that looks like an owl! Because she is so strongly imprinted on people, owl creatures are outside her area of interest. Also,

Second summer, Grayl and Roger Tory Peterson.

she has no experience whatsoever in hunting, and would probably have difficulty maintaining herself in the wild. The strongest reason for not giving her freedom in the wild, how-ever, is that she is a hazard to humans. Turned loose in a strange world, she'd probably fly to the nearest person as soon as she became hungry, expecting to be fed. Landing on the shoulder or head of an unsuspecting person could lead to accidental injury. For that reason alone, we would not dare to turn her loose. We knew all this, of course, well in advance of bringing her home. You can't take a young raptor from the wild, raise it with people, and then release it. A tame, human-imprinted raptor is a non-releasable bird.

Spring Thaw with Owl

Any bird that measures the
fall of a drop of water
studiously peering down at
the soft plink in the snow
then briefly glancing up
as if daring me to criticize
merits a lot of respect.

CHAPTER 2

Grayl Goes Public

GRAYL'S FIRST SUSTAINED PUBLIC APPEARANCE WAS AT A WINNIPEG shopping mall in April 1985. Backed by a Natural Resources display of large mounted photos of great gray owl field studies, she wowed people for up to twelve hours a day for six days in a row. She handled this schedule as if it were routine. The owl display was part of about thirty exhibits brought together for National Wildlife Week by Wildlife Extension Specialist Ted Muir. A variety of organizations participated: Purple Martin Club, Ducks Unlimited, Canadian Wildlife Service, etc.

Begun in 1947, National Wildlife Week includes April 10, the birthday of Canadian conservationist Jack Miner. Miner attracted international fame through his work with Canada geese at a sanctuary near Kingsville, Ontario. Less well-known was his abhorrence of birds of prey, as well as predators in general. Any hawk or owl that visited his sanctuary ran the risk of being shot or trapped. Thus, it is ironic that a live great gray owl should play a role in the celebration of National Wildlife Week. I'm not sure that Mr. Miner would have approved.

And what, I wonder, would he have thought of the great gray owl poster produced by the Canadian Wildlife Federation for National Wildlife Week, 1978? That poster showed a beautiful photo by Dalton Muir of a family of owls at a nest we studied in 1970. A quantity of those owl posters, donated to our cause by the Canadian Wildlife Federation, provided an important source of revenue for owl research. Trimmed and suitable for framing, they were offered for sale at our display. One graces our living room.

It wasn't difficult to enlist volunteers to help run the owl display. Friends and associates readily agreed to help, and put up with long hours dealing with the public with no complaints. Often, this meant answering the same questions repeatedly: Where did you get the owl? How old is it? Are her wings clipped? Does she bite? Will a flash bother her? When people at malls and in schools ask what we feed Grayl (a common question), I explain that we give her dead mice, mice that come from university labs where breeding colonies are maintained for research.

Because the display emphasized research and our interest in great gray owl habitat requirements, a lot of questions were asked about this aspect. I estimated that about eighty-five percent of our time was spent on education, and about fifteen percent on fund-raising. Getting people to contribute to research by purchasing posters and other items, or by direct donation, was part of the program. Several other display booths participating in National Wildlife Week attempted fund-raising, but our results, thanks to Grayl, far exceeded anyone else's.

Any live animal attracts attention, but the owl drew an unusual amount of interest. In fact, the pleasure of being in the owl's presence seemed a sufficient reward for the people staffing the display. Some volunteers were recruited on the spot. I let one young girl in a crowd at a mall hold the owl, partly to show people that anyone can hold her, but also because she had an appealing smile. Andria Cole, who was then ten years old, became a regular helper at the malls and other events, coming from her home in Altona, 98 km south of Winnipeg. Eventually, she spearheaded a fund-raising drive at her school in Altona. Hazel Dykes, an elderly woman who showed up one day at our exhibit, simply asked if she could help. She graciously dealt with folks for the rest of that week, and returned the following year.

All who have been involved in showing Grayl to the public agree that the most satisfying aspect is watching people's eyes light up when they stand and watch her. And watch her they do, some coming back again and again, some hurrying home and coming back with cameras, some coming back with friends to see the owl.

The owl is carried on a glove to which a leash or tether is attached, the other end being fastened to her jesses. I started out with a simple leather glove, but soon acquired a leather gauntlet that gives the owl more surface to grip. It also protects the wrist! Sometimes I pick her up barehanded. I do this when I want to weigh her on a scale, lifting her off her perch, shielding her eyes to keep her from flying, then carefully placing her on the scale. This sometimes takes a little time. Occasionally when, for some reason or other, she has slipped or dropped off her perch at a school, I may lift her back up with my bare hand. Ordinarily, she doesn't attempt to grip my hand when I'm doing this. She's even allowed me to do this in her pen, where she is normally more aggressive. For example, at 10:30 p.m., February 25, 1989, I noted: "Cold and windy. She is out on a perch looking about, intently interested in events outside her pen: the sky? tree movements? I can touch her almost anywhere. I pick her up and she does not tighten her talons on my bare hand. She sits on my shoulder for 20 minutes. When I first came out she was on the edge of her nest holding a large frozen mouse in one foot."

Travelling with an Owl

To transport the owl to and from various events, I built a car-perch, which consists of a foot-high small upright log fastened to a round plywood base. A short perch made from an oak branch is attached to the top of the log. From the perch in the back of my station wagon, she can see in all directions, and here is where she sits most of the time. Two small pink washable rugs are spread out over the base of the car-perch, as well as on top of any other gear in the back.

For immediate sanitary purposes, I spread sheets of newspaper on both sides of the car-perch, changing them when necessary. Usually, Grayl voids a blackish smelly mess within thirty minutes or so after leaving home. This stuff has a strong odour and I hasten to remove that piece of paper as soon as I can. My primary objective, however, is to keep Grayl from soiling her plumage. Thereafter, she voids the usual white, relatively odourless waste. For the most part, I'm happy to say, her plumage is impeccable.

Grayl's tether is fastened to the log. Thus, she can jump off the log and walk and hop about throughout the back of my station wagon. The tether is short enough so that she can't fly up in front of me when I'm driving. Sometimes, however, she'll perch between the front seats, right at my elbow. On one long trip she sat there for several hours, looking straight ahead out the windshield. If there are suitcases or boxes in the back, she may perch on them, occasionally even crouching down to rest, but always in a place where she can look out.

She clearly enjoys travelling in the car, often sitting up on her perch for long distances, and always alert. She turns to look at the people in almost every vehicle we pass, and often people look back, especially when I'm stopped at a light. I've seen some strange reactions. Since she invariably looks directly at the people in an adjacent car, doing this in a deliberate manner, she gets their whole attention. No dog looks so searchingly. Drivers and passengers alike do a double-take, point and exclaim, or even turn on windshield washers to gain a better view.

She balances easily, taking sharp turns and sudden stops – upon which she bends forward – effortlessly. One of the few things that sometimes bothers Grayl when she's in the car is a heavy rain. With rain drumming on the roof she often fidgets and appears anxious. At first, the sudden noise and movement of the front and back windshield wipers upset her, but she quickly learned to accept these novelties.

On Display in a Shopping Mall

Early in her career, when we took her to a mall for the first time, I perched her on a small wicker stool (borrowed from our home) set on top of a table. Her leash was fastened to the stool. This worked fine for one day. In mid-morning on the second day some silly kid reached in behind the table and pulled her tail. She didn't like it. She exploded off the stool in full flight over the heads of a startled group of onlookers. Such was the force of her flight that she pulled the stool along with her some six metres. We were lucky no one was injured.

Shortly afterwards I built the perch that I now take with us wherever we go. This perch is a T-shaped affair, 1.5 m high, made out of plastic pipe bolted to a carpeted wooden platform. The pipe and base come apart and are easily carried. The horizontal piece of pipe at the top of the perch is covered with carpeting to give the owl a comfortable and secure perch. To keep the whole thing from toppling over – and I had learned that if the owl decided to take off from the perch, she flew with enough force to pull the perch over – I

A big hit in the malls.

carry a covered plastic pail filled with sand for a counter-weight. This, plus a length of elastic between the perch and her tether, keeps the perch secure.

Once on her perch, she settles down and will stay there hour after hour. At any time in a mall, she's likely to close her eyes and doze, sometimes requiring a tap on the perch to get her to open her eyes. Touching her toes usually brings her to full alert.

For a long time, "Is it alive?" was the first question asked. This bird can sit very still for long periods. It's what owls do in the daytime, especially if they're well-fed. But this can be a problem. I well recall the day when a middle-aged woman moving past our display with a shopping cart suddenly shrieked and fell to the floor. She had assumed that the owl was mounted and was startled when it moved. Fortunately, the lady was unhurt, but after that episode, we added a promi-nent sign beneath the owl's perch: "Yes, I'm alive!" Still, de-spite the sign, we occasionally have people go away mumbling: "It's stuffed." Occasionally I kid with young people, advising them in confidence that "the owl is really electronic, built by NASA." And some of those kids return with friends to check it out.

During these long stints, Grayl often becomes restless, clearly wanting to stretch her wings, to move off the perch. I then take her on the glove and let her flap vigorously, an event that always attracts a lot of attention. Occasionally, we stroll around the mall, taking Grayl for a walk, as it were, briefly visit-ing other displays, even shops, inviting people to come to our booth. After ten or fifteen minutes of activity, Grayl is ready to return to the security of her perch, especially if we have been in the centre of a group of people.

In April 1991, while at Polo Park mall in Winnipeg, she delighted a large crowd by suddenly spotting and responding to a bird of prey passing high overhead. Nearly asleep one moment, in a flash she was alert and fixed on something be-yond our view through the large skylight windows far above

Tolerant of the young.

Natural Resources display, National Wildlife Week.

us. She leaned forward, head thrust out and tipped up, chin feathers protruding, peering intently and slowly moving as she tracked what we could not see. She was so intent on the unknown object that she could not be diverted, even by rattling her tether. I kept telling people to look for a hawk in the sky; eventually someone saw it and pointed it out to me. It was an eagle, circling at a great height, just barely discernible. Grayl continued to follow its course until it was out of sight. Then, just as quickly, she returned to her original relaxed pose, looking straight ahead. It was an impressive demonstration of her capacity for noticing things of importance in her world, notwithstanding the noise and distractions of a busy mall.

The presence of Grayl in a shopping mall is like a magnet, drawing people back again and again. On her perch, in front of an audience, she radiates serenity. There is this calm composure, this casual acceptance of people and noise that so impresses us. Something about her calm demeanour, so unexpected in a large bird of prey, surprises people. The steadfast stare, or half-closed eyelids, the nearly motionless manner, and smooth-as-silk plumage attracts people. At times, the exhibit booth is like a shrine with people coming to worship. People stare in wonder, mesmerized, for that moment caught up in this bird's mystical aura. For a brief moment, people of all ages drop their worries and concerns. There is a tendency to speak softly, despite the loud noise of the mall, and people visibly relax as they try to comprehend the mystique of a large owl that likes people. This is the secret attraction: this bird not only tolerates people, she positively enjoys them.

What a spokesperson for her kind! That curved bill, those long talons, that composed posture, these things offer a lesson in adaptability. Folks who have met this owl, and I use the word advisedly, come away with a new appreciation for birds of prey, owls in particular. The general attitude is not simply that they have seen an owl, rather, they have become acquainted, they have truly met this special bird.

Over her second year, Grayl appeared in public on fifty days, including twenty-three day-long sessions at malls throughout Winnipeg, and in Brandon and Portage la Prairie. In addition to promoting our own cause, we were helping to publicize a new educational program at the famed Oak Hammock Marsh. Several thousand people viewed Grayl during this busy period. She handled all events with increasing facility. The most difficult event involved going to the Red River Exhibition to promote Parks Heritage Day. We were located near a noisy band that bothered me a lot, but Grayl didn't seem to mind. Nor did she pay much attention to the sounds of barking from a nearby dog show. The sight of about twenty-five assorted breeds parading right past us seemed to amuse her. I suppose that from her point of view, dogs were dogs, as long as they weren't singling her out or showing aggression toward her. We only did the Red River Ex that one time.

Eyes that hypnotize.

Recognition

In April 1986, a great gray owl was depicted on a "Birds of the Prairie" lottery ticket issued by the Western Canada Lottery Corporation. I bought a few tickets, vowing to donate the money to owl research, but failed to win anything. Soon there were great gray owl pins, buttons, calendars, pencils, plates, T-shirts – all celebrating the species. The Cambrian Credit Union adopted the design of a great gray owl's face as a logo. For several weeks it blazed forth, enlarged about four times life-size, from the sides of city buses. Bold, colourful and huge, I thought it not an especially flattering rendition, yet it was unmistakably a bird of this species.

The results of our efforts did not go unnoticed. At an International Conference on Outdoor Ethics in November 1987, Richard C. Goulden, then Assistant Deputy Minister, Manitoba Department of Natural Resources, presented a paper that made reference to our tame owl. The proceedings of that conference include the following from his address:

New friend in mall.

Real *progress occurred when [a] highly-respected biologist made a rehabilitated great gray owl into [a] T.V. and public relations celebrity, touring shopping centres, fairs, outdoor festivals, and particularly public schools teaching about birds of prey and collecting money for research. Single-handedly, this initiative has done more to reduce wanton killing of hawks and owls than any other action... Success in this case is evidenced by the fact that one grade-six class raised more than $1500.00 for owl research over two years and the Great Gray Owl was confirmed as Manitoba's provincial bird.*

A Tolerant Creature

Of interest is the apparent variable response shown by Grayl to different people. Infants and small children, for example, hold her attention far more than do adults, and she tolerates more touching by small people. She may be dozing on her perch, eyes nearly closed, but let someone come by with an infant in a stroller and chances are that the owl will come

Her species – an emblem for Manitoba.

awake and peer down with tilted face. Little people hold a special interest for this bird and she has rarely shown any aggression toward a child.

Sitting quietly on the back of a chair in a school staff room while I enjoy a cup of tea, Grayl acts more like a person than an owl, looking up at each teacher entering the room. Once, when a visiting parent came in with a small baby in her arms, Grayl fascinated everyone by her attentiveness to the infant.

Even wild great gray owls have a more tolerant attitude toward young children. Once, Herb Copland and I took a bird we had just captured into a U.S. customs office at the Manitoba-Minnesota border to show to the staff. They excitedly phoned some friends and we were shortly demonstrating the bird to a roomful of people. The bird, which I was holding upright against my body, appeared calm; I kept saying that it was a wild bird and people shouldn't try to pet it. I winced when the youngest child pushed forward suddenly and pressed his hand against the owl's face. That dangerous contact drew no response. Again, when we invited a group of children sledding on a hill at the Black River Indian Reserve to come see a newly-captured owl, they pressed around us, reaching out and pawing the bird. Surprisingly, the owl accepted this rough handling, and I was even able to raise the facial disc and show the kids the owl's ears.

The apparently tolerant response shown by Grayl to an older blind girl at a mall may relate more to the direct way in which the girl brought her hand forward to touch the bird. The girl ran her hand over the owl from top to bottom unscathed. Grayl has tolerated a lot of touching, though I usually limit it to a light touch on the face above the eyes or on the breast. When she wants to, she can give a good nip, and a few people have been surprised in this way. The trouble is, she looks so cuddly. Thousands of people have touched this bird. Over the past few years, however, I have stopped inviting people to touch her. Touching can be handled in small groups, but when there are large numbers of people crowding about, it is hard to control its extent. Adults are the worst, for they have more temerity, wanting to pat the top of the owl's head in the same way one pats a dog or cat, sometimes pressing down with enough force to make the owl crouch down. I keep telling people that she's not a pet, and that birds don't really like being petted. Generally, my impression is that Grayl tolerates touching, but I've never been sure that she likes it. One person at a time is not bad, but in a group situation, with people all around, Grayl shows signs of unrest, so I try to avoid having people crowd in around her.

A more photogenic bird is hard to imagine. Grayl's calm beauty sends people back home for their cameras. Media people and professional and amateur photographers use cameras of all kinds to try to capture images of this popular bird. Often, I'm asked by people who have seen the bird earlier if she has changed colour. There seems to be a general impression that she looks different, but I think this depends on the lighting. In

Famous owl lady meets lady owl, Kay McKeever holding hands with author as Lady Grayl drops Kleenex.

the subdued light of a mall or school, there is an overall gray appearance, but in better light, fine features are apparent. Her face, for example, has a bluish tinge and the white markings seem brighter. Under really bright lights, as in a TV studio, her colours are enhanced, she glows, is resplendent. Seen on TV, she almost looks like a different bird. On a few occasions, artists brought their sketch pads to our mall display and worked away, inspired by this imperturbable owl. I like to think of all those pictures and photos in various homes, with people of all ages cherishing images of Lady Grayl.

With Grayl as the centre of attention in a mall, we received donations, and sold a variety of great gray owl souvenirs: posters, plates, books, buttons and prints of Grayl – all for owl research. People were generous; it was the presence of the owl, and numerous well-informed and friendly volunteers, that made this aspect so successful. During a National Wildlife Week we made as much as $3,000 in six days, but it was often gruelling. I developed a number of pat routines. After someone had praised the owl's beautiful appearance, I'd say, modestly: "Of course, I do her hair." It always got a laugh, except once when a dour older man countered with: "Well, that's your problem, ain't it." I had no reply.

If someone says "What a beautiful pet!," I quickly point out that "No, she's not a pet; she's a research and educational tool." "Yes, but you get to keep that beautiful bird." To which I add: "Sure, I have the privilege of worrying about her welfare twenty-four hours a day."

And I do worry. It bothers me that one misguided miscreant with a pellet gun could so easily destroy this charming bird, as has happened at Kay McKeever's secluded owl rehabilitation centre. It's possible that a dog or fox could harry our bird to injury or death, as has happened to raptors being rehabilitated by other friends.

Things could happen even when we're on tour. A few years ago I parked outside a small rural school, leaving the owl in the car while I went inside to let the teacher know I had arrived. As I went back outside, an unknown man informed me that, "That owl could sure fly!"

"What?" I asked, "It flew?"

"Yes, when I let it out of the car it really took off!" I ran to the car in panic, but there she sat, quite secure. The guy was just pulling my leg, but ever since then I've kept the car locked or had someone on hand to ensure against the unlikely occurrence of someone turning the bird loose.

Driving with Grayl in the car, I feel a special responsibility. If the owl's mission is to help people better appreciate her kind, my mission is to get her safely home. I'm especially careful after surviving one accident. Driving home after a long day at a Winnipeg mall one year, we hit a deer. Crashed into a deer would be more accurate. A full-grown doe had come out of a ditch and in front of the car just as I looked to the other side for deer in a field. It was like hitting a brick wall. The deer ended up in the opposite ditch, upside down and dead. Fortunately, the owl, although shaken up a bit by the sudden stop, was fine. The front of the car, however, was wrecked. The first car that came along stopped. Seeing me standing beside my car, this nice lady got out and, putting one hand on my shoulder, said: "Stop crying, and turn off your ignition!"

"But my car," I cried, "And I've got to get the owl home, and tomorrow morning I'm supposed to take the owl downtown for a live TV program!" Dianna Sahulka had seen us at the mall, and happened to live close to me. She said that if I'd put the owl in her station wagon, she'd drive us home, and in the morning take us downtown. And so she did.

A Gathering of Owl-watchers

The momentum generated by our success with the tame owl, the excitement of our various activities, and the vigour with which the radio-telemetry study was pursued, led to the idea of bringing together ornithologists who studied great gray owls both in Europe and North America. Discussions with friends and colleagues soon led to a decision to broaden the scope, to hold an international conference on all owls of the northern forest regions. Thus was conceived the Northern Forest Owl Symposium, the first of its kind. The symposium was sponsored by the Manitoba Department of Natural Resources, the University of Manitoba, World Wildlife Fund Canada, The Wildlife Society and the U.S. Forest Service.

Held in Winnipeg for five days in February 1987, this event attracted 160 registered delegates from twelve countries. What a gathering! February was chosen because we thought it might be the best time of the year to see great gray owls on a field trip. That has been the case for most years, but on this occasion none was seen. However, Lady Grayl was on hand, much to the delight of the delegates. She proved to be as appealing to these owl specialists, several of whom had worked with great gray owls, as to the general public. A number of people had their photo taken beside this cooperative bird.

Owl symposium, Åke Norberg, plenary speaker, from Sweden.

Although the symposium covered some sixteen species of northern forest owls, great gray owl images appeared on the covers of the program, the abstracts, posters, etc. There was even a great gray owl mascot, a costume nicely designed by Ingrid Campbell to portray this species. This huge bird was featured at an evening social. I danced with the creature, not realizing that it concealed Bill Koonz, a fellow biologist. The biggest surprise for me, however, occurred at the opening ceremonies when my boss, Merlin Shoesmith, as part of his introductory remarks, read a poem that I had written about the great gray owl. Lady Grayl sat quietly on her perch near the podium as he read the following poem:

Large Owl

"The bird is not as big as
it looks" say those who measure
with a finger
poked through feathers to body.

What nonsense! The owl is entire
of itself, massive in a coat of
soft plumes, and the perfect outline
of its round head is what the bird is,
no more, no less.

Each feather's tip is sensitive
to touch, a part of the bird
as leaves are part of a tree
transient as molted feathers.
Twigs, buds and hidden roots
make a tree; the maple with its
distinctive shape, the symmetry of
a spruce...who would question where
the tree begins?

All those feathers can be moved,
compressed, fluffed out
expressing changing moods or
responding to weather.

True, its light feathers
are easily ruffled by
the wind, as a girl's hair,
another part of its charm.

If the size of a bird
is judged by its spirit
then this bird is even bigger
than it looks.

CHAPTER 3

Grayl at Home

By June of Grayl's second summer, I was involved in studying her behaviour and especially her moult, the business whereby a bird changes plumage. Studying her moult required that I visit her pen daily from late April through August in order to pick up feathers. For this and other reasons of convenience, that summer I took over permanent care of the bird, transferring her to a large flight-pen in my own yard. The Scriven family expressed regrets at the move, but their pen was soon being used to house a golden eagle that Renate was rehabilitating.

Now I could spend even more time with Grayl, visiting and observing her daily. To further the development of a bond between us, that fall I hauled a small mattress into her pen and spent several nights there in a sleeping bag. One cold night in February I announced that I was going to sleep in the pen with Grayl. As I recall, it was -20°C or thereabouts. Ruth thought I was daft. Still, it gave me an opportunity to see what it was like out there in mid-winter. I lasted until 3:00 a.m., when I decided I'd had enough.

Grayl's pen is 6 m long, 3.6 m wide and 2.4 m high. It has a dozen different perches, a large shallow pool, a nest platform, and a roof at one end. The floor is covered with pea-gravel. Situated at the far end of our yard in a small grove of trees, the pen has areas of sun and shade. From here, Grayl has a view in practically every direction. Judging by the number of birds of prey she has spotted from her pen, including several eagles and hawks flying high overhead, she sees past the trees.

Grayl lives here throughout the year. When people express surprise that she lives outside even in the winter, I am quick to remind them that, after all, wild owls all live outdoors. As long as they have protection from the wind and food available, owls can withstand the most severe temperatures. One would think that in really cold weather, she would perch in a corner with two solid windproof walls and a roof, but invariably Grayl may be found in a breezier position, one where she can see what's happening. In the middle of more than one stormy night I have found her sitting exposed, head covered with snow, blinking at me as if wondering what I'm looking for. Some frosty mornings her face will be a mask, her breath causing a layer of hoarfrost to form over all but her eyes. Only when we see her upper eyelashes coated with frost do we realize how long they are. Sometimes only the eyelashes are frosted, the result of vapour off her eyes.

Equally surprising is Grayl's ability to adjust to rapid changes in temperature, moving indoors for one to three hours, then back out to her pen even in extreme subzero weather. As far as I can tell, it bothers her not at all. In the same way, she travels in the car, summer and winter, then calmly goes into hot schools.

Mice for Dinner

Frequently, school children ask if they can see the owl eat a mouse. I explain that this is not feasible because she eats in the evening, which is only partly true. One could regard this interest in watching the owl eat (or even kill, as well, for I'm sure that's what some of them have in mind) as morbid fascination, but the behaviour of any predator with prey is fascinating.

Although I have often watched Grayl eating, I still find this behaviour compelling. In very cold weather, for example, when it gets down to -20°C or -30°, I often give her a mouse in the morning, when she's quietly roosting in her corner. I go into the pen, reach into my pocket and offer her a mouse without disturbing her. Under these circumstances, she takes the mouse and swallows it without budging from her cold-weather perch. It's a moment of peculiar intimacy – at times I feel like a male owl feeding a mate.

If I sit on a stump in her pen and place a mouse on my knee, she'll come to get it, landing on the mouse with one foot, then picking it up with her bill. If I hand her a mouse through the wire screen from outside the pen – and a number of visitors have done this – she walks along the length of the perch and then stretches out to reach for the mouse. She takes it in her bill, then holds it, head upright, in one foot. Often she pauses, as if she's considering her next move. If she doesn't simply gulp it down, she often tears off a bit of skin from the nape of the neck. After a moment, she swallows this tiny morsel, seemingly relishing this initial taste. Then she takes the mouse by its head in her bill, pupils enlarging, feathers flaring out from around the bill. Just before swallowing the mouse whole, she crunches down on the head. The nearly regular pattern of this behaviour suggests that it is related to the business of automatically killing prey.

Taste and smell in owls are relatively unexplored topics, but these senses are probably more functional than is realized. Once, a drop of blood from a mouse applied to the outside of Grayl's bill led her to smack her lips, as it were, opening and closing her bill and moving her tongue about. It's at least an indication of the sensitivity of the bill.

Even large mice may be swallowed in two or three gulps. A hungry owl can swallow a surprisingly large animal; voles are pretty big, but great grays can swallow even pocket gophers whole. Still, Grayl usually eviscerates large mice, especially when she's only moderately hungry, leaving strings of gut for me to remove when I come across them in her pen. She removes the gut with the skill of an experienced chef, first peeling back a piece of skin from the chest and neck region, then nipping off bits of flesh which she swallows thoughtfully. After cutting loose the intestinal tract (more than 30 cm long in a medium-sized lab mouse), she pulls at it, lifting her head, until the entire length is drawn out and breaks off. This is done ever so tidily. Usually she watches it fall to the ground.

The mice always go down head first, and I've noticed that Grayl is careful to pick up mice by the head end. Even very small mice get this treatment. This makes sense, for the reverse position would mean moving the mouse against the grain, as it were, forcing the hair backwards.

On a few occasions, I've offered her a mouse in the backward position (tail first), just to see if she'd notice. As I lift the mouse up to her, she reaches for it, then hesitates, waits until I reverse it, and then takes it. Or she takes it, and adeptly reverses it herself before swallowing it. This kind of observation makes me doubt the suggestion made by two scholars, as mentioned in Larry McKeever's book, that owls can't see well at close range. (On March 14, 1994, for example, a feather fragment lifted off her shoulder in the morning breeze. She watched the single hair-like filament closely as it wafted past her face.)

If Grayl is hungry, she'll take and swallow up to three mice, one after the other. Or she may swallow one or two, then hold a third one in her foot for several contemplative minutes before dropping it. Sometimes, she switches feet, taking the mouse out of one foot with her bill, putting that foot down and raising the other foot to hold the mouse. There is a neat relationship between the two feet and the bill in handling things.

Usually, and especially in warm weather, I don't take time to offer her mice, but just leave them on a platform inside the pen; like an old-fashioned milk-chute, it opens with a little door on the outside so that we can leave mice for Grayl without entering her pen. That's how my wife feeds the owl when I'm not home.

Grayl may not eat all the mice at once; sometimes one or two are left and fed upon during the night or the following day.

In warm weather, a dead mouse quickly attracts wasps and flies; before long there may be fly eggs everywhere. I try to keep mice from sitting on the shelf too long, and I regularly brush away the fly eggs. A mouse that is slightly ripe doesn't seem to bother Grayl; after all, this must happen in the wild when mice are left on the edge of a nest. Rather than risking her health or attracting carrion insects, I remove older carcasses, preferring to waste a few. I also make sure that there are no mice littering the pen, for they could attract a skunk, raccoon or fox, animals we'd rather not have coming around.

In winter, the mice she doesn't eat right away quickly freeze and are suitable for food for some time thereafter. I've never known Grayl to swallow a frozen mouse whole. Usually, she takes them off the shelf to the top of a stump where she holds the mouse in one foot and carefully bites off bits and pieces. It is a meticulous operation; she works slowly and studiously, seeming to savour each piece. The appearance of frozen flecks of blood or flesh on the snow, on the stump or on the feeding shelf, show me where she's devoured one more frozen mouse.

On December 17, 1992, at -23°C, we watched her from the house as she nibbled at a frozen white mouse on her stump. Hunched over, feathers loosened, head down as she worked on the mouse, she looked immense against the snow. Between bites, she raised her head to look about, first this way, then that way. It is a matter of security. In the same way, wild owls feeding on the ground keep an eye out for danger.

Feeding is serious business, requiring some degree of concentration. One time, when I was watching her closely as she took a mouse from me, she was startled when our neighbour's dog suddenly barked, a sound she ordinarily ignores. Ten minutes later, when I went out for a closer look, she was crouched low on the stump, motionless, resting, face covered with frost. She paid little attention to me. Apparently, she was warming the mouse with her body. This has been reported for the boreal owl and other species, but not, so far as I know, for the great gray owl. Then she lifted up and resumed feeding on the partly-skinned mouse carcass which she clutched in one great feathered foot.

Going back over my notes, it intrigues me to see that right from the beginning, when I first started taking the owl in a car (fall, 1984), her greatest sign of stress occurred when she was returned to her pen. This curious behaviour still occurs today. She appears comfortable at a school, sits upright and seems relaxed on the way home. But nearly every time when I return her to the pen, she suddenly subsides, showing signs of apparent stress, drooping her wings and panting for a few minutes. It seems that when she's out in public, or away from her pen, she is controlling her mood, keeping up appearances. She doesn't really relax until she's back home, safe and sound, in her pen. This suggests that, to the owl, the pen represents maximum comfort and security. It is reassuring to me to think of the pen in those terms.

It is not surprising to find that Grayl likes to get back to her pen. By now, she has lived here for nine years. It is a familiar place. Birds returning to a territory in spring, after months on the wintering grounds, similarly must feel some satisfaction or excitement. The house wren that comes back to the bird house in which it raised a family in the previous year is drawn by its memory to return to that particular site. That first burst of song in spring, though initiated by hormone levels, probably reflects some level of the bird's comfort in finding itself back home.

Sunbathing

I know of no more startling image of a bird than a robin or a flicker sunbathing. From an alert, upright, watchful pose, these birds prostrate themselves upon our lawns, wings and tail spread out, heads tilted back with a dazed expression, and mouth open to the hot sun of summer. At first glance they look mortally wounded, but of course when approached they quickly fly away. Sunbathing is an instinctive act, birds responding at certain times of the year and day to the sun's warm rays, and no doubt with beneficial effect. Oil from a bird's oil-gland (located above the base of the tail), when spread on the plumage and exposed to sunlight, is changed to Vitamin D. A small amount of this altered oil is ingested during subsequent preening, thus providing a source of this needed vitamin.

Sunbathing has only infrequently been observed in owls in the wild; a single observation of this behaviour in the scops owl, for example, was recently published in a major journal. E. Mackrill saw the owl sunbathing on a horizontal branch of a large shrub on August 6, 1983. My only observation of a wild great gray owl sunbathing involved a female brooding young in a nest on June 2, 1970.

Grayl often sunbathes in the typical rigid fashion, more or less, sprawling upon the gravel in a sunlit area of her pen, wings spread out upon the ground, head tipped back, motion-

Sunbathing.

less. This happens especially in June and July, usually at midday. My notes from May 7, 1989, noon, mention that "she walks out into the sun, spreads her wings and lies down, faces the sun, tilts her head back until she is looking straight up, but her bill is closed. From time to time she turns her face, sunning all sides, as if enjoying the sun. Do we feel the same urge? This is the first time this year I've taken my shirt off; after I did so, I was pleased to turn and see her sunbathing. She did this for eight minutes."

After reviewing my notes on several observations of this behaviour, I conclude that her bill usually is closed during the siesta, and her eyes may be either partly open, almost closed or closed. Once, May 26, 1990, at 11:45 noon, after coming upon a robin sunbathing in our yard, I went to Grayl's pen and, yes, found her in the same ecstatic state. A few days later, on June 1, when it reached 32°C, Grayl was sunbathing at 4:00 p.m., an unusually late time. She flew up onto a stump and from there tilted her face up to the sun. On two other occasions she performed on a perch. On July 1, 1986, for example, she sunbathed on the ground at 12:30 noon. Then at 2:00 p.m., while on a perch with her back to the sun, she turned her face over her left shoulder to face the sun, and raised her chin up until her head was resting on her right shoulder.

Grayl's pen has been visited by red squirrels on numerous occasions. One even has a den beneath a nearby brush pile, and sometimes I leave sunflower seeds in Grayl's pen just to attract the squirrel. I have also seen the squirrel go into her pen for a drink, entering at the top and scampering down a long slanted perch to the edge of her pool. Grayl seems to enjoy the company. Other birds venture in to drink from her pool, or to steal feathers, and once I saw two blue jays, presumably young ones, harassing her inside the pen. Cottontails and chipmunks live here and even deer have walked right past the pen; not bad for a city lot. I have also seen a neighbour's house cat perched on top of the pen, but this is definitely not something I encourage.

Since this tame owl has an interest in people, our neighbours' and my wife's gardening activities are watched closely. Jets pass overhead, there is an almost constant sound of traffic from a nearby major thoroughfare, power lawnmowers grind away, but all these sounds have little interest for the owl. She has a fine ability to ignore them.

Centre of the Storm

For weeks there may be no sign of alarm from other birds in the vicinity of her pen, then, suddenly, something happens. One Saturday in late June, a visitor, looking at the owl for the first time and noticing the absence of birdlife, guessed that the owl had "scared all the birds away." I assured her that wasn't the case, pointing to an active house wren's nest in a birdhouse only 2 m from the pen. But, except for the chattering wren, it was very quiet. The next morning, however, a robin's scolding brought me out to the pen. "Speak! Speak! Speak!," with flashing upraised tail and nervous wing flicks, the robin called repeatedly. I approached the owl in the pen to see if this would reduce the robin's evident anxiety, but at this the robin came even closer, as if my presence only encouraged her. Now I could see the sun lighting up the inside of the robin's bill! The intensity of the robin's emotion, the bright details of her plumage, even the saliva glistening on her tongue – what a treat to see a bird so close.

The robin had evidently just discovered the owl, for she carried on in this excited fashion for fully fifteen minutes, at one time attracting five other robins. The clamour of all these birds adding their own excitement eventually attracted a great crested flycatcher which called loudly, but kept out of sight, as well as a male northern oriole. The oriole flew into a tree near the owl's pen, whistled a few times while methodically hopping about from branch to branch busily picking off insect larvae, but otherwise it showed little interest. What a noisy affair!

The owl ignored all this, sitting up on her highest perch, calm, imperturbable – just silly robins carrying on.

The five robins that had come over to see what all the noise was about appeared to be trying to tell the excited robin that the owl in the pen wasn't a big deal, nothing to get excited about, just the old owl that lives there. One by one they lost interest and moved off, leaving the single scolding robin by herself. Perhaps the robin had a newly-fledged young – always a nervous situation – somewhere nearby. When the owl stretched her wings and made two forceful flights the length of her pen, the robin moved up closer, whereupon the owl went to roost at the back of her pen. Still the robin carried on, moving behind the pen to keep the owl in sight. Eventually she lost interest and flew away. Silence returned.

On August 20, 1990, I am standing in the owl's pen in mid-afternoon, with this bird on my shoulder. A peaceful moment, I look at the shadowed trunks of nearby aspens, thinking this feels like a woodlot, though I can hear a background noise of traffic, a kind of surf sound which the owl, I note, ignores. My reverie is broken by the arrival of a flicker, a dashing youngster on a limb above us. The owl turns its head to look at the flicker and at once the stage is set. The flicker parades, standing upright on long legs, dropping its head to left and right in rhythmic motion, a swordsman flashing a sabre. Its bill stabs up and down as it inches closer on its limb above us, and its "Whick! Whick!" startles the shadows. Its loud calls also bring a host of other birds. In a moment we are surrounded by four more flickers (an entire family), two orioles, two blue jays, a white-breasted nuthatch, five robins and a few house sparrows. The owl glances at each new arrival, giving but short attention to each, though the dash of a blue jay screaming above its head gets a long, hard look.

All these birds alarm each other, the noise increases, the scolding takes on an ominous tone and finally the owl reacts. Her excitement is manifest as she leaps off my shoulder and onto a perch with wings held upright, and then hops off to another perch, from one side of the pen to the other, caught up in the thrill of all this fervent attention. Tired of standing still so long I move a little and at once the birds are startled. They hadn't noticed me before, but now they disperse rapidly, only the blue jays hanging in, scolding, though their calling has lost some of the earlier excitement. In the midst of this I note a curious call, grating, froglike, a sound new to me, like someone trying to scratch a piece of glass with a stone; it is one of the blue jays. I hear it again just before the jay moves off.

And now the owl is quiet, bemused, nonchalant. It was fine bedlam, such excitement to be the centre of attention, a kind of joy, judging by her behaviour. I am deeply stirred, pleased to have shared this moment, to have been in the centre of the storm, at such close range and under circumstances permitting me to observe her every action and reaction. For this period of time I am the true observer, my anxieties forgotten, my self discarded, caught up in the owl's feelings which I strive to share.

Nocturne

January 5, 1989, midnight. The owl is sitting up high, facing southeast. Her attention seems riveted on something up high. She turns abruptly, moving her head from left to right and back again, as if following the movements of birds. But there are no birds. When I enter her pen I am surprised that she remains facing away from me; it is the first time she has done this. Usually, she turns around at once to confront me. This time she remains facing away, even when I approach her. She continues to watchfully scan either the tops of nearby spruce trees or the sky, I can't tell. It is -12°C, overcast, calm, a hint of snow. There is icy frost on the feathers over her bill and I can see her breath! I touch her back tentatively; normally this brings her around in a hurry, but she ignores me. Curious to see how far I can go, I run my hand down her back, along her folded wings, down her tail – she ignores all this! Even when I gently tug on the tip of her tail she continues her silent watch. This is impressive. She is a different bird than the one I'm used to.

When she turns around, finally, she looks at me only briefly, large pupils giving her a gentle, benign look. But my poking and prying bother her little and she keeps looking around, at times swinging her head suddenly as if a sharp noise compelled her. When the dog, running happily loose in the snow in the night, comes running by, she turns and looks down at him, but without any alarm, then returns to her vigil. I am awed by her attentiveness, puzzled by the forces that drive her, impressed by her seeming spirit of wildness. Is this what the wild owls are doing at this very moment, I wonder? Perhaps the well-fed ones? I should stay out here all night to record what she does, but I'm tired, so I call the dog and go off to bed.

When I return in the morning at 7:15 a.m., she is sitting in the same place, facing the same direction, apparently still doing the same thing. I am stunned by the awesome thought that this bird can do this through the night. What incredible attentiveness. She is never bored. Every little movement, each little sound, patterns of branches against the night sky, the sound of the wind, these realities and presumably many others beyond our scope excite and interest her.

When I think of the long-distance movements of some of our radio-marked owls, as much as 800 km in less than three months, I think that these birds have capacities we are just beginning to glimpse. And this tame bird, no less, still has inherited patterns of response, feels things, has inner compulsions. I am witness to a spirit. I realize what little there is beneath this feathered form – a small body, long legs, not a great deal of mass, the brain – no, what we have here is the spirit.

Brooding a Pitcher

On average, I bring her indoors for a few hours once a month, letting her roam at will from her perch in a room with two couches and down a hallway into a sewing room that also contains a freezer. We turn her loose in the family room, one of three rooms built into our basement. To move from one room to another, she flies down a hallway, brushing her broad wings against the walls, or she goes on foot. This surprises people, for she strides along with a springy gait in a purposeful manner. When she runs, she looks surprisingly agile, pushing forward with each leg as she moves along. It is something rarely seen in the wild. She begins on her customary upright display perch, moves to a similar low perch in the same room, then flies or runs down the hall to my wife's sewing room. Here she spends time either perched on the freezer (her usual landing spot) or on top of a sewing machine, but she invariably ends up perched on the end of a small shelf above the freezer.

Looking back from her shelf with pitcher.

Moving the pitcher closer.

It must feel good.

It took me some time to realize that she was attracted to an object on the shelf. My wife keeps a small white pitcher full of distilled water on the shelf, using it to fill the steam iron. At first I thought that the owl was perched beside the pitcher co-incidentally to sitting on the shelf, but one day I found her hunched over the pitcher. While it seemed unlikely, it looked as if she was deliberately resting her chest upon it.

Then, on March 24, 1990, I tested this. After seeing her crouched over the pitcher, I forced her to move away from it and even moved the pitcher back from the edge of the shelf. Soon, she began pulling it toward herself and part way under by reaching out and hooking her bill over the edge of the pitcher, nudging it underneath. Then she sat with one foot on each side of it. There was now little doubt that she was brooding the pitcher. I hesitate to say incubating the pitcher, but the way she reached out and pulled the pitcher toward herself with her bill so that she could nestle on it was much in the manner of an incubating bird moving an egg into position.

Lacking eggs or young, Grayl finds a substitute in the form of a 10-cm-high porcelain pitcher. She seems to derive some comfort from it, returning to it on numerous occasions. Even during the non-breeding season she shows an interest in brooding the pitcher, so it's not simply a matter of hormones. In mid-November 1992, for example, I brought her indoors after she had been outside in her pen for a month. Soon after, she flew to the shelf by the pitcher, then reached out and moved it over so that she could rest on it. But she soon moved away.

Grayl has also cuddled up to similar objects under other circumstances. Twice I have seen her hunched over a cup that happened to be sitting on luggage in the back of the car where she could get at it.

Has she ever laid an egg? The question is often asked by school children. She hasn't, presumably because she lacks suitable stimulation. When adults ask this question, one of my standard lines is that there's a limit to how far I'm willing to go to keep this bird comfortable. I also explain that she's not with a male, so if she did lay an egg, it would be infertile and wouldn't hatch. Besides, I'd rather she didn't lay an egg; because if she had one, she'd want to sit on it, and then she wouldn't let me take her out to schools! Moreover, egg-laying would involve physiological stress, and with her workload I'd rather avoid this situation.

That Grayl has a reproductive urge is clear. Hormone levels are apparently on the rise in great gray owls as early as January. This presumably accounts for Grayl's unexpected delivery of the distinctive double-noted territorial vocalization on January 12, 1990. My notes state that "at 12:15 noon, when I stood a dozen yards from the pen, she suddenly began giving the territorial call: 'oo-hoo, oo-hoo, oo-hoo,' rather soft but distinct, with her throat puffed out, perhaps 15-20 times in succession. This is the first time I've heard her give this call."

I suppose the reason she so seldom gives the call is the lack of suitable stimulation. Birds respond to internal stimuli to a certain level, but often external stimuli are needed to elicit displays or calls. At times she shows a genuine interest in the nest-platform in her pen, visiting it, scratching down through wood chips to the screen bottom, sitting in it and carrying things to it. A few examples will set the picture. On January 8, 1991, at 10:00 p.m., I found her sitting in the nest, very still. When I went into the pen to check, she quickly stood up as if embarrassed. The next morning, I found her again sitting in the nest.

On April 20, 1987, after preening or grooming her with my fingers for several minutes, she came onto my shoulder, preened my ear, nibbled at my glasses. "When I take her to the nest, she crouches on my shoulder and watches, then, when I place my hand in the nest, she quickly jumps into the nest and turns around to face me, all puffed up and indignant. She is then aroused and aggressive or assertive." Often, from February through April, she becomes aggressive toward me, her behaviour apparently being related to nesting. Wild great gray owls begin to establish territories in late January and early February, and females begin laying in late March and early April.

Once, when Grayl was being especially antagonistic, I went so far as to place a white hen's egg in the nest. My notes of May 4, 1987, record that "she watched intently, but there was no apparent change in her belligerent attitude. When I removed the egg, which she could see, she was visibly upset. When I went to leave the pen, she attacked me, forcing me to fend her off with one hand. Prior to the attack, she vocalized like a female owl disturbed at the nest, giving a menacing 'Who-hoo-oo-oo!' She did this three times." Sometimes her attacks were unexpected and even hazardous, leading me to ask raptor specialists what I should do. In the end, I decided to just work harder to win Grayl's confidence, entering her pen cautiously, and always trying to gauge her mood.

Communication

Grayl has learned to accept both dogs and cats at fairly close range. We no longer have a cat, but our present dog, a Brittany spaniel named Buster, and the owl are on good terms. Mutual respect covers it well. She even tolerates him in her pen; I now let him go in there without fear of risk to either one. Sometimes, when Grayl is in the house, she will perch within a metre of Buster, always watchful but unafraid. Should the dog move unexpectedly, the owl may flush (suddenly start to fly); generally, Buster carefully averts his eyes and tends to move more slowly when she is present. It is interesting to note that the bird "understands" the averted-eyes signal; that is, she responds appropriately to that gesture by the dog. Most wild creatures recognize this submissive sign.

On one occasion, I noted that the owl perched low and less than 2 m from Buster, who was lying down, for twenty minutes. All that time she watched him steadily, blinking now and then, a slow deliberate blink, which gave her a grave expression. One eye can blink by itself, but usually this slow blinking is with both eyes at the same time. Grayl could have moved away, but she stayed there, that close to the dog.

At times when Buster comes up to her pen, Grayl reacts to him more vigorously than usual, elevating her plumage and glaring at him as if she doesn't know him. It is a temporary thing, very brief, and not easily understood. I think she enjoys assuming that aggressive role, putting on an act as if momentarily caught off guard and needing to assert herself. It suggests that her reactions are more complex than a simple stimulus-response allows.

Of course, Grayl's reaction to dogs varies with circumstances and individuals. Recently, I stopped to visit friends in the country on my way home from a school visit with Grayl. The overly-friendly dog at the farm came running up rather spiritedly. Though Grayl didn't get off her perch in the car, she responded in much the same excited way that she reacts to eagles. She raised her feathers, thrust out her wings, and hooted loudly. This surprised me, for she had seen this dog at close hand on at least two previous occasions. It is possible that her reaction was altered by some inner compulsion apart from just seeing the dog up close, perhaps by her experience at the school.

The only place that this tame owl shows aggression to humans in a serious way is when she is in her pen. Then she can be dangerous. Of course, if she's annoyed, say by someone repeatedly prodding or teasing her, she will peck or bite or even attempt to grab with her talons, but by and large she's gentle and tolerant. Inside the pen, however, she has attacked with vigour the few people I've invited in to visit her. This happened six times before I came to understand that she would not tolerate visitors, other than myself, inside the pen. Fortunately, no one was hurt. Once, when my poor wife went into the pen holding a dead mouse in her hand, the owl at once attacked her, hitting her on the back of the neck as she turned away. As Ruth – more scared than hurt – withdrew in alarm, the owl stared malevolently at her. It took the owl a few minutes to settle down, such was the extent of her arousal.

Particular things that annoy her include touching her toes, her tail and her wings. Any kind of teasing, especially when she's in her pen, is likely to upset her. I can bring on a strong protest just by running two fingers along her perch toward her. A dead mouse moved toward her in the same way is an offense. Grayl wants respect, and as long as I adjust my behaviour to meet her needs, we get along well. Once outside her pen, however, Grayl is an entirely different bird, tolerant of everybody. And anyone can hold her on the glove. On several occasions, I've invited students to do this, always without any problems.

Lacking the complex facial musculature of mammals, birds have relatively unexpressive faces. Thus, the erection of plumage, the movement of wings and tail, and vocalizations play a major role in communication. Of all birds, however, owls probably have the widest range of facial expression. This is owing partly to their flat faces, forward-facing and large eyes, and responsive pupils. Also, the facial disc can be slightly altered in position, and the head plumage can be erected or compressed, as is true of nearly all birds. In owls, a surprising change in expression can occur, all relative to the bird's state of being. This is especially so for the eyes.

Eye expressions, resulting from positions of the flexible eyelids and variable pupil size, are surprisingly variable; some probably serve in communication. When Grayl is comfortable or relaxed, her pupils enlarge. As she gets more relaxed, the pupils get larger until only a little of the iris is visible. When she closes her eyes, it's the lower eyelids that come up to cover the eyes. Sometimes, at the last instant, the pupils expand fully as the lids close. With alarm, apprehension or fear, the reverse happens, the pupils contracting until they are quite small. This indicates intensity of feeling or concentration. It can be elicited temporarily by something as slight as a hand brought toward her. In her pen, standing close enough to feel her breath on my nose, I can watch her pupils enlarge slightly as she reacts to sounds, a distant car horn, a door slam. It is a sensitive measure of her attentiveness. The size of her pupils is a good indication of her emotional state or mood, or level of concentration, just as is her whole posture. We judge her mood, and the significance of her behaviour, by observing the context, by seeing what follows a particular display.

Of course, the pupils also operate by reflex action, responding to changes in light intensity, getting smaller in bright light and very large in dim light. There is also some suggestion that pupil size may relate to visual requirements, the smaller pupil size aiding in seeing things up close. When Grayl first reaches for a mouse that she is about to eat, her pupils go small, then enlarge as she swallows. Taxidermists take heed; too many mounted owls have the eyes fully round, as big as they can get, even bulging, the characteristics of a staring bird, one that is alarmed or antagonistic. A much softer, relaxed look is achieved by letting the upper lids droop a little.

In the live owl, the corners of the eyelids are not aligned horizontally – the outer corners are slightly higher than the inner ones. When the lower eyelids are raised, as in a sleepy bird, this gives a squint-eyed, slightly quizzical appearance. Grayl often gets this look when she's puzzled, concerned, considering or hesitating. The squinting look can come and go rapidly.

Behaviour in the Pen

In late March or early April, Grayl exhibits a restlessness, presumably associated with nesting activities, which later gives rise to pseudo-attack or predator-strike behaviour. Most commonly, she pounces on a stack of large bark fragments which I arrange for her on a stump. Once this behaviour begins, often in early to mid-May, it is a daily occurrence, lasting until fall. She demolishes the stacked bark sometime in the course of a day or night, and daily I replace them. If I'm home, we may do this several times a day. It is a task I take seriously, placing one piece atop another as high as I can, and dribbling a little gravel on top of the arrangement for auditory effect, all under her watchful eye. Usually she waits until I've gone away, but on a few occasions I've watched her pounce. One or two quick strikes with elevated wings for balance and feet out in front as she arrives and, with a clatter, my artful arrangement is scattered around the stump.

This owl is full of surprises. One day she showed me that even in play she can be dexterous. On October 15, 1985, at 6:30 p.m., according to my notes, she picked up a piece of bark that was about 36 cm long, pecked at it, then carried it with one foot onto a stump, then up onto a vertical pole, holding the piece of bark by the end in one foot. There she transferred it from her foot to her bill and vice versa three times. Then she flew up onto a nearby horizontal perch about 5 cm in diameter. After moving the slab around a few times, somehow she ended up with it laid crosswise on the perch. Then, with her

A snug haven.

feet resting on top of the bark slab, and one foot on each side of the perch, she balanced as it teetered first one way, then the other! A remarkable sight.

Once, when I was trying to approach Grayl to snap the tether onto her jesses, she slipped off her perch from behind. She caught herself with her bill, hooking it over the perch and then, by flapping heavily with her wings, she got back up onto the perch. I've seen young owls, fledglings that can't fly, use their bill in this fashion, just like parrots, but I hadn't previously seen an adult owl do this. I was surprised another day when she took something I offered her and held it off the ground with her bill. It was a full-sized broom I'd been using to clean her pool. It had a wire loop at the end of the handle and when I pushed that toward her, she seized it. After she dropped the broom, I hastened to take it in the house to weigh it. She had been holding a 650 gm weight, exactly half her body weight that day (April 27, 1987).

Grayl's weight is something I've monitored almost monthly. To weigh her, I have to get her to stand on top of a scale. To do this, first I have to get her onto my bare hand, then I transfer her to the scale. It takes a little time. Usually, I do this in the house, but occasionally I take the scale out to her pen. By the end of her first year she weighed about 1.5 kg. Thereafter, her weight varied from a low of 1.1 kg to a high of 1.7 kg.

Annually, her weight decreases over summer and peaks in early winter. Usually she is heaviest through the winter months. The weight changes relate to food consumption, but this is based on her own urges, since food is available to her at all times. I don't mean that I leave an unlimited quantity of mice in her pen, but that the number of mice I give her is based on the number she demands. She demonstrates that she wants more food by sitting by her feeding tray, peering into it at times, or by giving a begging call. I don't like to waste mice, so I limit the number in her food tray according to what she consumes.

Grayl's annual weight changes appear to be a natural periodicity, presumably related to the onset of winter and the need to build up fat reserves for harsh weather. Possibly the weight gain offsets increased difficulty in obtaining prey. The weight changes may also relate to the reproductive period, to a need to establish adequate reserves for egg production. Because wild-captured great gray owls are routinely weighed, the information obtained from our tame owl has wide implications and provides a substantial basis on which to interpret weights of wild owls.

Early on, Grayl selected another stump, one that sits in the area of her pen that is open to the sky, as a place to carry out a strange exercise. I'm not sure just when she first began picking away at the decayed surface of the stump, but by biting and pulling at the wood with her bill, by clawing and jerking with her feet, she has managed to make an irregular cavity which is now about 20 cm deep and 18 cm wide at the top. During the past two summers she has deepened it by 13 cm. If there hadn't been a hard knot near the centre, the excavation would probably have progressed faster. The process was speeded up by moisture and decay, but the hole really resulted from her efforts. Even today, new bits of debris on the edge of the stump tell me she's been at it again. And occasionally I have seen her in action, studiously reaching down with one long foot to bring up material from the bottom.

As I write at our dining-room table, I can see her at this game, jumping down onto the stump with wings held high overhead, thrusting her foot into the cavity. It occurs to me that she often does this in the evening, after I have placed mice in the feeding tray. It seems to happen after a long period of inactivity and before feeding, the exercise of stalking and pouncing normally carried out in the wild.

In May 1993, I noted that she put her face down inside the cavity to bite off pieces of wood. On May 30, at 4:30 p.m., "she is on the stump, drops a stone and twig inside. A little later, she plays her game, stands up high on the stump with wings elevated, then drops down, reaching with one foot deep inside, right on down until her chin rests on the stump, flat on her belly, reaching – she is, in effect, grabbing at a mouse under the snow." All this is interesting in itself, but considering that great gray owls may nest in the hollow tops of broken trees, especially in the western U.S., one wonders whether owls using such nest-sites ever improve them through this kind of activity.

For the past year or so, I've been involved with her in another game. Daily, I place two rounded stones on each side of the top of the hollow stump, and one or more twigs either on the side or across the opening. And she removes them, carrying the twigs off some distance or dropping them beside or inside the stump. The stones are usually dropped beside the stump, though often one is carefully dropped inside. When I replace these artifacts, she always watches attentively. I have also found feathers, leaves and once even one of her regurgitated pellets down inside the stump.

She also carries things, mostly sticks and stones because they are available to her, to a nest-platform that was installed when the pen was first built. It's simply a shallow, screen-bottomed tray about 1 1/2 m off the ground at the back of the pen. Although we have no evidence that wild owls bring anything to their nest-sites, this exercise suggests that it could happen.

Two years ago, when I first saw a scooped-out shallow depression in the fine gravel in one corner of the roofed end of her pen, I was puzzled. This hole was first observed on March 26, 1990, and was 45 cm long, 20 cm wide and up to 5 cm deep. That first time, I assumed that my dog – which I occasionally let into the pen – had scratched it out with his hind feet. The gravel from the excavation was piled up against the wall. I smoothed it out, but the next day it was there again, in exactly the same place and in the same way! I raised the question at the office, wondering whether a red squirrel, an occasional visitor in the pen, would do this, or what?

My notes from that day read: "...it looks like a scrape made by a bird, say, scratching backwards – it is shallow, and gravel has all been moved in one direction – see photos." I moved the gravel back into the hole and smoothed it out with my hand, still puzzling over its origin, looking at the owl, wondering how she could do this.

Two and one-half hours later, in the evening, I spied on her at some distance from the pen and saw her perform. "The mystery is solved!" my notes say, "At 6:55 she left the high perch, flew around the corner to the back of the pen and struck the ground lightly with her feet. Five minutes later she did the same thing again, hitting hard on the same spot, then flying back to her perch and repeating this act five more times, thus making a wide furrow in the gravel floor of the pen. Each time she hit, gravel flew up noisily against the wall, no doubt a part of the effect she enjoyed. She had discovered a new game."

Almost daily, for the next month, she did the same thing, excavating what I so carefully filled in, but not once during this period did she attack the bark pile. Not until April 25 did she return to that activity. Thereafter, she ceased digging in the gravel. Not until late March, a year later, did I find a sign of digging again. For days thereafter, I filled in the hole daily, and daily she dug it out again. Remarkable, in 1994, she again attacked the bark pile for the first time on April 25! The timing baffles me.

In April 1991, I came into the pen and found a shallow furrow in the gravel, perhaps 15 cm wide, extending for about 2 m. This resembled nothing I'd previously seen, and, except for the fact that it lay along the same course she took in pushing out the gravel near the back wall, I could hardly ascribe it to her. But I assume she had made a series of strikes of about the same strength to make that shallow trench. An amazing bird.

Recently, I've noticed signs that occasionally in winter, after snow has fallen, she plays this game belatedly, hitting the snow and/or the gravel in the same place at the back of the pen (late January and late November 1993). And a few times, especially during mild days in February, she has plunged her feet into a snowbank in the pen.

In these "attacks," whether pouncing on the bark pile or striking the floor of the pen, she seems to enjoy her "play" activity. In both cases, her behaviour seems somewhat similar to that of an owl pouncing on prey. In the same way, she has peeled the bark off all the perches in her pen, repeatedly picks at the carpeting on her perch, and pulls at bedding and cushions in the house. It is her way of asserting herself, using up excess energy, it is something to do. With the onset of cold weather in late October, and especially with the first serious snowfall, all these play activities come to an end. It is winter, and Grayl now appears more serious; she sits with compact plumage, appearing to relish the cold, eyeing the snow with interest.

A *Night Bird*

For the most part, Grayl is generally alert all day long, sometimes because she doesn't have a choice, leading us to think that she sleeps at night as we do. But with nightfall she becomes even more alert, a different kind of bird. She is, in fact, a night bird, but because she is often so active in the daytime, there is this false impression. The difference in her attitude toward being touched by me tells it all. Typically, when I poke a finger at her in the daytime, she shows some signs of annoyance. If I persist, she may bite my hand, sometimes drawing blood.

At night, she lets me do almost anything I like. She sits up high, looking around, giving me scant attention when I approach and reach out to stroke her head and face. Reaching inside her plumage, thrusting fingers right into the base of her neck, probing underneath and caressing her legs, even lifting her wings and fondling her toes. None of this can be done in the daytime without risking a hard nip. But at night, she is so busy checking on things, she disregards my forced intimacies. I can carry on in this fashion as long as I like, with impunity, and I enjoy it greatly. This was my inspiration for a poem written in October 1989.

Tame Owl

Standing in the owl's pen
at midnight
face to face
close enough to note
the scent of warm feathers...
the sky is clear, half a
moon hangs in the south.
I think I feel
the owl feeling, something
in the way she turns
her face upward
staring at, at stars!
This owl is looking
at stars, and briefly
I glimpse starlight
reflected in her eyes.
Though she sits still and calm
yet in the play of
shadows from the
pen's slatted roof
her plumage seems to
undulate...it is more
my poor vision.
Standing so close to
this bird that a day ago
drove me, frightened,
from her pen in her
mad nesting mood
I've become wary.

Now, in this
midnight hour
sensing her subdued mood
I dare to stand close
wanting her acceptance
so, humming her little song
still uncertain about
our relationship until
she murmurs back to me!
Oh you great bird
you're talking to me!
Awful, I think, to have
felt your rage, but
oh, to be accepted again...
so run my fingers softly
across her shaded face
to find her bill
so well defined
a little warm, and
know a kind of bliss
when she nibbles softly
at my fingers.

Evening, it seems to me, is the most exciting time of day for great gray owls. Or that level of light, perhaps, for it is on dull, dark days approximating evening conditions that we see more owls out. Today, December 26, 1992, my seventieth birthday, I take two mice out to Grayl at 4:45 p.m. It is -17°C, and snowing lightly. I find her on the perch by her food tray, her watching perch. She can't be too hungry, for I gave her a large mouse in the morning, but she takes two from me, one right after the other. There are no preliminaries; she nips each one, bites down on the skull, swallows rapidly. All this takes place inches in front of my face, for I am face to face with her in her pen.

For the next ten minutes I stand there, enjoying her perfect plumage, the startling liquidity of her golden eyes, puzzled by her behaviour. She is studying something out there, turning her head quickly every few seconds and staring, or listening? There is no other movement, first to the right, then to the left. I count seven seconds, five, eight, four, ten in each position. It is fascinating. What, I wonder, does she perceive? I listen carefully; I hear a train whistle, and the low rumble of cars on the track, a dog barks, a distant siren sounds, another dog. Grayl tilts her head up, sharpens her glance at a spruce spire that moves in the wind, resumes her steadfast monitoring of the evening, to right and left. Finally, she turns her head to look, or listen, behind, through the slats of the pen, then she reverses and peers ahead, over my shoulder. Night sounds, the hiss of snow, boughs in motion, perhaps somewhere an owl.

Little did I realize, when I wrote the previous paragraph, how close to the truth I might be. Oddly, the very next evening, at -30°C, Grayl showed me a new bird, a first record for a sighting from our yard. Shortly after I fed her at 4:30 p.m., she resumed her watchful mode. A few minutes later, she tipped her face upright and to the north, then went into the tall, narrow posture: alarm response to a raptor. I searched the sky, nothing, turned back to see her tracking steadily, chin out-thrust, intent, now looking east. I continued to search the sky, then saw it, a gull?! No, a snowy owl, very high, beating steadily and rapidly southward on a strong wind. So, from within the pen, she sees the sky, looking past the slatted and screened pen, through spruce boughs, to what matters to an owl. Sometimes I think that she must hear such birds, though that seems unlikely.

Often I find Grayl picking out raptors soaring high overhead. This has happened several times when I've been watching her in her pen or on a perch in our backyard. One moment she's looking straight ahead, mildly interested in a scolding house wren or some movement of a bough. The next moment she's staring up at the sky, with that "Aha! Another raptor,"

Something in the sky.

look. I'm just about convinced that under these circumstances she hears them before she sees them. Is this possible? Some sound that she can detect that goes unheard by us? Otherwise it is hard to understand what moves her to suddenly tilt her head up and fix her eyes on a hawk soaring more than a hundred metres overhead. It is true that she often scans, as if checking the sky, but there have been times when she has turned away from some inspection of an object to turn her head upwards immediately to an overhead raptor or other bird. I asked Swedish ornithologist Åke Norberg whether this was possible. Professor Norberg replied: "I doubt that the owl can hear the aerodynamic noise of a hawk overhead. We do not ourselves hear a soaring hawk at close range, which we should do if the owl does so at a much longer range. One possibility could be that the hawk [soaring high overhead] produces low-frequency sounds [vocalizations] below our lower-frequency limit of hearing, and that the owl hears these low frequencies... ."

While trying to determine how Grayl spots raptors (and gulls and high-flying jets, etc.) passing overhead, I've spent some time standing beside her. After she's fixed on something in the sky, I peer and crane my neck, searching for whatever she has spied. Looking up through the slatted roof and tree branches makes it difficult to see anything, but the problem is compounded by my inability to remain still. The owl, however, sits remarkably still, secure, solid, unmoving, for as long as she likes. It makes it a lot easier to see something overhead. It's part of her secret.

January 9, 1993, 10:30 p.m.: It is -35°C; a clear, cold night with a full moon, so bright the stars are dimmed. The dog and I go out to feel the night. While the dog eats snow, I go and sit beside Grayl who is roosting in a shadowed corner. She is busy watching the night, and ignores me. She looks repeatedly to right and left, then looks up through the slatted roof at the moon in the east. For a moment I am puzzled by a white spot on her head, a spot of moonlight. Though she doesn't move on her perch, she is as active as ever. This is her sleeping place, her nighttime roost; has the moon awakened her? Her world is all around, visible, audible, and she takes it in, turning her head quickly from point to point, and back to the dazzling moon.

It annoys me that I can't get her attention. Here I am, sitting in front of her, touching her, but she is busy following the movements of the dog who's come looking for me. I whistle, open the pen door, admit Buster, who cheerfully trots about in all corners, sniffing, lifting a leg. Grayl acknowledges his presence with a subdued snap of her bill, drawing her tail forward and spread, hunching a bit, giving two more soft snaps as Buster stops beside me to look up at her. I let him out, watch as he runs off in the moonlight, go back to trying to get a response from this strange bird. I talk to her, nudge her, no reaction, she's still busy watching the night, listening in all directions. I gently insert one bare finger into the feathers of her throat, probing until I can feel her body, noting how the down surrounds and holds in heat, her body functioning, warming us both with mouse energy. Stroking her back, caressing her silky head plumage, I'm thinking how well prepared the owl is for cold nights, how this kind of bird evolved to the state of perfection found at this moment, how this particular bird and I have met, have bonded.

When Buster comes by again, I reluctantly leave, slightly disappointed because I'm unable to elicit the little bunt of the bill against my hand that is her way of signing off. So I leave her, wonder bird, there in the night. Walking up the moonlit path to the house, I am aware of the cold. Ruth is still up when I come in, concern for my well-being on her face. There are spruce needles caught on my white toque, a suitable token of the night.

Nowadays I find myself interacting with Grayl as if she were more than a bird, as if she could understand me. It's silly, but there is some sort of relationship between us, such that she greets me when I come to her pen, a soft cooing or humming sound. I either reply in kind, or speak directly to her. This bothers me. I wouldn't want anyone to know that I'm talking to a bird. Yet it seems natural. So I say hello on my daily visits to pick up moulted feathers, to search for a pellet, or to give her fresh water.

It goes beyond that. I visit her often, mostly for the good feeling I get from this curious relationship. These daily visits are partly an effort by me to provide her with company. Rarely a day goes by, at least when I'm home, that I don't visit with her for several minutes, day or night. But waving goodbye when I walk away is undoubtedly a sign of my dotage. Still, I do this more and more often, holding up my hand, then closing it once or twice. Hands, of course, are strong aspects of people. The open hand pushed toward her elicits a strong aggressive response. She doesn't like it, and reacts accordingly, bristling a little and leaning forward in obvious annoyance. So she watches the hand wave with some attention. So far, I haven't let anyone see me do this.

After another nocturnal visit, I wrote the following:

Sleepless Night

Cold electric ecstasy of
Northern Lights writhing foggily
across the sky
Orion perched high overhead
on a sleepless night
in late October.
Four in the morning is nothing
to this tame owl who
watches me with amusement
quietly staring down
at me when I murmur greetings
a low, soft hum, her call
and she lets me touch her
anywhere I please
her calm, composed demeanour
at this hour reminding me that
she's a night bird, sits
watching the sky move
interpreting cosmic creaks
rustles on the ground
faint sounds as a sudden breeze
lifts a bough; her gentle
acceptance of the night, of me
a quiet balm.

CHAPTER 4

Grayl Goes to School

IN THE FIRST YEAR OF PUBLIC EXPOSURE TO THE OWL, THERE WERE numerous requests to bring the bird to schools, but I turned most of them down in favour of hitting the malls and other situations where there were large numbers of people. I was intent on increasing public awareness and on fund-raising in support of our research project.

Not until a teacher at Selkirk's Centennial School inspired his grade-three students to raise five hundred dollars for us did I realize the fund-raising capability of elementary school kids. Merv Haines' young protégés got on the environmental bandwagon, collecting bottles and cans for recycling. A huge laminated poster with a marvellous drawing of a great gray owl went up at the school. Later it was used by me for several years as part of our mall display. Drawn by grade-three student Lonny Gnitzinger, it read: "Give a Hoot, Help Raise Money for Great Gray," and "Bring some bottles/Baking too/Bring some books/and toys will do." I was pleased to take Grayl, then six months old and fully grown, to school. I held the bird on a glove and let the kids have a look at a "real, live owl." As a special treat, I let them all come up and touch the bird, a reward for their successful fund-raising effort. Twenty of Merv's students received an award: "The Order of the Gray Owl Feather," appropriately decorated with a feather.

Over the next several months, Centennial School kids worked even harder at fund-raising, ending up with a thousand dollars, an incredible feat. It took no effort to persuade me to return to the school with Grayl for a special presentation. A representative from the Premier's office read a message from Premier Howard Pawley congratulating the children for their contribution to owl conservation. Laurie Mustard, host of a kids' TV show called "Switchback," also attended; when he walked into the gym, the kids recognized him and cheered. The whole pleasant event was covered by a CBC-TV cameraman and a reporter; it made the national news.

Fund-raising by school children reached another high level when Carman Elementary School teacher Carole Anderson organized an effort involving kids in her school and three other schools in adjacent communities. Local merchants donated gifts for a raffle and the kids sold tickets. Who can resist a schoolchild's request to buy a ticket to help save owl habitat? For the students, the reward is a sense of contributing to the betterment of the environment, doing something for wildlife. As well, of course, there is the promise of a visit by Grayl, this famous owl. More than five hundred students assembled in the gym at Carman School, those from outlying schools coming by bus. With a government representative on hand (my boss at the time, Merlin Shoesmith), I gave a talk and demonstrated the owl. Then, in a special ceremony, two grade-three students presented me with a greatly enlarged, but valid, cheque for more than two thousand dollars. The affair was filmed by CBC-TV for a later program, and a live CBC radio broadcast took place over lunch in the teachers' staff room. What fun! Of course, it would be unfair to Mrs. Anderson and the students if I failed to mention that the students learned something about owls as part of the project.

Not all school tours yield so much money, but we aren't in this for money alone. Before I take the owl to a school, students are expected to study owls in some depth, as well as to do some fund-raising. When these two aspects are followed, there is a commitment that makes young people more knowledgeable and involved. An owl school-tour package that I send out to teachers includes a list of recommended audio-visual materials available on loan, including great gray owl films, a video and a slide-set. The real benefit of a visit, then, is the preparatory learning that takes place before we come to the school. Thus, the owl comes as a reward for learning. The more that students have learned about owls, the more effective the visit.

One of the best dialogues occurred when I took the owl to a grade-four class in the inner-city area of Winnipeg. The thirty-five students had baked cookies which they sold in their neighbourhoods to raise our required basic fee of one hundred dollars. The money was handed to me in a shoebox just as the kids had collected it. These kids had worked hard fundraising, but they had worked equally hard at studying owls. Each student had chosen a single species to study, not just great gray owls, but several species of owls. The depth of study may be judged by the question one boy asked: "Dr. Nero, could you tell me, please, the clutch size for Blakiston's fish owl?" Remember, this was a grade-four student. "Hm," I replied, "I'll tell you the clutch size if you can tell me its scientific name," thinking that would hold him. But, no, he had memorized the name! In the end, I had to fumble to come up with a guess as to the clutch size (number of eggs laid) of this little-known southeast Asian owl.

Roberta Frolich's class had studied owls in relation to other subjects in the curriculum, developing skills in math, writing, sociology and art. The classroom was filled with examples of their owl work. We had a stimulating discussion lasting nearly an hour. The session was video-taped by another teacher, thus providing a permanent record of the visit.

A Worrying Man

Taking the owl to a school is for me always an adventure, nerve-wracking, but satisfying. I worry too much. As a person who suffers from anxiety (don't we all?), I take heart from something the late Louise de Kiriline Lawrence wrote in Mar: A Glimpse into the Natural Life of a Bird, her book about yellow-bellied sapsuckers:

Nervous tension and stress act like power units that release new bursts of energy into the living system. This is the animation of life. It pushes the organism from one situation to the next, from struggle to rest, and forward to meet new demands upon its powers of adjustment, of adaptability, of grasping and assimilating new versatilities.

But one has to get to the school, in some cases driving a considerable distance, at an appointed time. Even leaving home takes an effort, putting the gear in the car – perch, weighted bucket, posters, prints, owl buttons, newspapers, brochures, etc. – and if it's for an overnight stop, a whole lot more. Some things can't be rushed; getting the owl from her pen and into the car partly depends on her attitude.

Whenever I approach her pen, grey carrying-glove tucked under my arm, she is quick to notice. With the tether wrapped around the glove, and the glove tucked under my arm, you wouldn't think it so noticeable, but it is something she has learned to look for. Usually she reacts when I'm still some distance from the pen, bristling (raising her head plumage), hooting and bill-snapping. Her aggressiveness increases as I get closer to her; her eyes get funny, well, the pupils go small, and she may hiss and try to bite as I reach for her jesses. Sometimes, I think, she puts on a show of false resentment, glowering, bill-snapping and flying away from me just to maintain her sense of independence. Even at a school, where she is so well behaved, when I go to take her off the perch, she invariably gives a few token bill-snaps. (Similarly, when our dog comes by her pen she tilts her head, apparently pleased to see him, then often gives one soft bill-snap. It is as if she suddenly needs to assert herself just a little.)

I've learned to unwrap the tether in an unhurried way, eyes averted, talking softly to her, before trying to snap the tether onto her jesses. There are times when she's reluctant to let me do this. All I can do in that case is to follow her around in the pen, coaxing, until she stops long enough to let me hook her up. It's the one thing I can't force. A few times, I've been scratched by the owl when I moved in too close too fast. The look on my wife's face when I walk past the house, an owl on my glove and blood on my cheek, makes me keenly aware of her concern. She now checks me over every time I come out with the owl. But I've learned to be patient with Grayl, usually giving myself enough time so that we don't need to hurry.

Upon arriving at a school, there is always a little panic in my mind, a struggle to find out where we'll be located, to recruit help to bring in the gear and the owl, all the while fending off questions that I'd rather handle during the talk. It's impossible to walk into a school with the owl without drawing a lot of attention and questions.

Not until the owl is on her perch in a suitable location, with everything on hand, microphone working, etc., can I relax. And, perhaps, to some extent this applies as well to Grayl. Usually within ten or fifteen minutes after she has been moved onto her perch, she suddenly ruffles all her plumage, shaking her head like a wet dog. This comfort-shake, as I call it, means that she is comfortable and is settling down. Sometimes she does this in the middle of a presentation and it always gets a big laugh. In the car she has a certain stature: upright, calm, watching. When she arrives at a school and is finally settled on her perch, she seems bigger. Some subtle difference in her posture gives her greater presence – she seems in her element, beneficently looking down upon a hundred faces.

Grayl's capacity for sitting quietly on her perch means that I can leave her there for long periods of time. I don't mean unattended; she's rarely left alone in a strange place. When I first set up in a school gymnasium, I'm reluctant to go off for tea in the staff room until I can find a student to keep an eye on the owl. But as long as I have her in sight, I can relax, more or less. Even in the dark, when I'm showing slides, her behaviour is nearly impeccable. Several times, she has sat through an evening banquet in a room filled with noisy diners, then, unruffled, has remained on her perch while I gave an hour's slide-talk. Occasionally she has created a diversion by hopping down off her perch onto the floor or an adjacent table or even a stage. This doesn't bother me if I'm the one giving the talk, but I'd rather she didn't do this in the middle of someone else's speech. When this happens, I may move her back onto the perch, though usually, after a little exploration, she flies back up onto the perch by herself. School kids find it hilarious when Grayl suddenly drops down off her perch onto the floor; a little undisciplined behaviour excites them. Besides, it gives them a chance to see her walking. Once, she broke up a school audience by flapping onto a stage, then scrambling hard on the slippery boards, pulling vainly against the elastic tether, trying to get a purchase to move another few inches away.

For most school tours, I first talk for about twenty minutes about Grayl's history, her age, measurements, food, living quarters, and especially hearing and vision. Where I can, I relate these things to wild owls and their capabilities and needs. As much as possible, I direct my remarks toward the owl on the perch, since, after all, everyone's watching her anyway. Should she stretch, yawn, pant or preen, I interrupt myself to explain what she's doing. If she turns her head around to look back over her shoulder, I direct everyone's attention to her position. One of the commonest questions is: "How far around can she turn her head?" My standard reply is, "Straight back and about ten degrees farther," whereupon I often launch into a discussion of the immobility of owls' eyes and thus their need for a flexible neck. And then I may ask the kids to try to look at each other without moving their eyes. It creates an interesting stir. It is the fixed position of an owl's eyes that gives it such a staring look. Most birds and mammals move their eyes now and then, but an owl can only look straight ahead. To change its field of vision it has to turn its head.

There is, of course, a limit to how far an owl can or will turn its head to look at something. Recently, while watching Grayl look over her back, I noticed that if something catches her attention just beyond her vision she quickly reverses position to look back from the opposite side. Having rotated to her right as far as she could turn her head to look backwards and away from me, when I touched her on the left side of her head she swung her head completely around to the left to see what had touched her.

It often happens that when I'm being introduced, say, by the principal, Grayl will upstage that person by suddenly ruffling her plumage. More than one person has nervously wondered why all the kids have suddenly burst out laughing. When I'm speaking, I tend to stand off to one side so that I can keep an eye on the owl.

My talk is followed by a ten to fifteen-minute question

Face to face.

period, an affair that requires someone to help identify students, and to help me understand what's being asked, for my hearing is a little less than normal, and youthful audiences can be noisy. Questions vary: How high can an owl fly? How old is she? How long will she live? How big are her wings? How can you tell a male owl from a female? If students have seen one of the films or the video on the great gray owl, then they often ask me to demonstrate how the owl preens. In the films, I show how an owl that we've captured instinctively preens my hair when I lower my face and offer the top of my head to the bird. Grayl won't preen me, I explain, because she's imprinted on people, therefore she's not afraid of me or any other human. It works with wild owls because they feel aggressive toward us, we're enemies or creatures to be feared, and when we lower our heads we're being submissive, and that gesture elicits preening, the opposite of aggressiveness. The question makes a nice opening.

Although I'm unable to elicit a preening response from Grayl by offering her the top of my head, she does respond to preening by hand. That is, when I move my fingers over her face, pressing fairly firmly (assuming she's in the right mood) especially around the base of her bill, she responds by tilting her face and running her bill around my hand, gently nibbling at my fingers, eyes closed, feathers spread back from her bill. This works well, especially during the time she's growing new feathers on her face and around her bill. Bouts of mutual facial preening between paired great gray owls are common, occurring, as photographer Michael Quinton has so nicely documented, throughout the breeding period. Certain small, colourful feathers concealed at the top and bottom of the facial disk (and referred to in Chapter 5) may be exposed in the course of facial preening. Could these feathers possibly function in some way at this time?

A Foot Fancier

Something about people's feet interests or bothers Grayl. This first came to my attention during a photography session in our backyard. Grayl was sitting outside her pen on a tamarack pole put up for this purpose. Of course, she's fastened to this perch by her tether which is snapped onto a large staple on the side of the pole. This allows people to see and photograph her at close range, for once she's on this perch, she's entirely approachable. After a team of two photographers had taken movie and still shots for more than half an hour, Grayl suddenly leapt off the perch and pounced on one man's shoe. No harm was done, of course, though we were all a little surprised by this obviously aggressive act. This happened again on at least two other occasions, though there didn't seem to be anything distinctive about the shoes or the people. When Grayl is in her pen, she often looks down at my feet when I stand nearby on the outside. I've decided it is mostly in response to noise when I move slightly.

Recently, I saw her respond directly and repeatedly to a person's foot. This happened in a classroom at Winkler school on January 15, 1993. After some discussion, I let the owl loose on the floor so that the students could see the owl walk. It's something I can let a small group of people experience. On this occasion, I let the kids come forward for a good look at Grayl hopping and walking. Toward the end of the session, one little girl began to tease Grayl, pushing one foot toward the owl and back again. Grayl caught onto the game, to the girl's amusement, and began trying to pounce on her foot, jumping a foot or two across the floor. The kids thought it was hilarious. I don't suppose that this was any more complicated than any teasing game involving a dog or a cat. And apparently Grayl enjoyed it.

Perhaps, when she drops down onto a photographer's foot, she is just relieving some tension, attacking not the person, but a remote part, a harmless gesture. On the other hand,

Grayl vigorously attempted to strike the foot of a girl standing by her pen on March 7, 1993. Several times when the girl slid her foot along the snow toward the pen, Grayl flew to attack, striking with great force against the wire screen, talons fully spread, wings upright for balance. On two occasions Grayl thrust both feet through the fence, once almost hitting the girl's foot. All this appeared to be simply an aggressive act, the sort of demonstration of assertiveness that we've learned to expect from Grayl in her pen.

For single classes or small groups of students I also have some tactile aids or hands-on items that I pass around, including a plaster cast of a dead owl's skinned head. This allows me to demonstrate the depth of plumage on Grayl's head. Simply by holding this object up near her head and describing it, students can see the difference in size. In small groups, I often add to this impression by inserting a pencil vertically into the feathers on top of her head. Like a child wearing a parka with the hood up, the owl's head appears larger than it is. Åke Norberg commented on this aspect as follows: "The head and face are enormously large for the size of the owl, and the huge facial ruffs and discs are extremely well developed. Indeed, the whole face acts as an external ear, collecting sound over its entire surface area." The heavy feathering of the head may also provide protection when snowplunging and, of course, the plumage keeps the bird's head warm. Looking at photos of Grayl taken outdoors, as well as photos of wild owls, I am reminded that the hooded effect also shades the eyes, an important feature for hunting over snow in the daytime. However, the snowy owl, which is even more of a daytime hunter, lacks this feature.

Owls, like other birds, have a kind of third eyelid that cleans, moistens and protects the eye when needed. Prominent in owls because of their large eyes, this bluish-white membrane sweeps across the eye diagonally from the inner corner to the outer. At times, it moves across the eye slowly. Occasionally, a student who may have passed by Lady

Grayl just when this nictitating membrane was over her eye asks about her "blue eye." It is one more feature I can show a class by lightly touching Grayl's face near her eyes. Just blowing across one of her eyes stimulates the reflex. In a few species of birds, e.g., the common grackle, the nictitating membranes are flashed in a display function.

In March 1993, I visited an inner-city elementary school. When I walked past some students with Grayl on my arm, one small boy pointed up at her and said emphatically: "Nictitating membrane!" I was astonished. Thuan Truong, an eleven-year old boy of Vietnamese ancestry, had never seen a live owl before. He and his grade-five classmates, however, encouraged by teacher Teresa Campanelli, had studied owls in depth. Still, how had he managed to spot and identify that fine detail as I carried the owl past him? In the end, I spent more than two hours with that class, coming back another day for a second rewarding discussion.

Depending on the age level of the class, I can talk about a variety of things. With small groups, I'm also able to show the kids Grayl's ears. This may sound strange, but since we talk about owls' keen hearing, I like to let them see the owl's ears. Grayl usually allows me to raise one side of the facial disk, the feathered flap that overlies the ear, thus exposing the external ear opening. With Grayl on the glove, I can just manage to do this with my free hand, bracing my thumb on her bill and lifting the flap with my fingers as I walk around the group. A most tolerant bird!

Owls Eat Horses!

With youngsters, there is a limited attention span and I try to keep on a light vein, though I don't talk down to my audience. To focus on the bird, and to get the bird to move around a bit, I run through a routine involving a toy horse. It works. At Brandon Mall in the fall of 1985, Grayl showed a strong reaction to a stuffed animal toy, a turquoise horse with a long pink mane and tail known as "My Little Pony." After watching her display to the toy horse with the usual aggressive crouch, intense fixed stare with small pupils, and pecking, I put the horse out of sight under the table. Several minutes later, after a period of distraction, reacting to people, etc., in which she was her usual relaxed self, she went back to crouching and staring at the place under the table where the horse lay concealed. My notes read: "She suddenly recalled the presence of the horse and reacted to it...she remembered where it had been placed and how she felt about it."

There's more to the story. I had borrowed the toy horse from a little girl who stopped to look at the owl. After letting the owl react to the toy, I gave it back to the excited child. She went off with her mother, but twenty minutes later she came back – she wanted me to keep the horse for the owl. Her mother, who was as surprised as I was, said: "I can't believe this! She hasn't let go of that horse since we gave it to her!" A few days later, after deciding that I owed the little girl something more, I described the incident to a Brandon newspaper columnist. Charley Hope wrote an article about the story, asking for help in identifying her name and address. Kitrena Low, then nine years old, and I exchanged several letters.

Kitrena's toy horse is still a feature of every classroom visit. Grayl and I follow a little routine. I get the kids' attention by telling them to watch closely while I perform a scientific experiment. "Watch the owl, see if she does anything special!" Then I go off to one side to where I've previously set down a large leather satchel, reach in and pull out a plastic bag enclosing the toy horse. The kids still don't know what's coming, but they can see that the owl has turned her head and is watching me closely.

With as much of a dramatic flair as I can muster, I pull the horse out of the bag and point it toward the owl. The sight of the toy horse, which many kids instantly recognize, brings forth a bevy of nervous giggles, whereupon I caution the kids to keep an eye on the owl. Then, with the horse in my hand and my arm held out like a fencer advancing on an opponent, I move toward the owl, shaking the horse so that the long tail and mane toss about. Grayl responds on cue, staring fixedly at the horse, and then, as I get closer, lowering her head in an aggressive stance. This is my cue to get her to swing about so kids on the other side of the room can see what's happening. Circling in front of her with the horse pointed toward her like a gun, I get her to turn around. By now, she's as low as she can get, crouched forward, head down to the level of the perch, glaring at the horse. Usually, I go back and forth two or three times so that everyone gets a view of her posture.

In the final stage of this silent duet, I push the horse forward until the owl bites at it. This always elicits a roar of laughter which increases to a climax when I hold the horse over her head, thus getting her to stand up to bite at the horse. Something in the sight of the owl stretched upright, face uppermost, meanwhile snapping at the toy horse brings

Full house.

down the house. We've done it again. Moving off to one side, I announce: "This proves that great gray owls eat horses!" Kids love it. But I'm always careful to conclude by lowering my arms and the horse, and dropping my head just enough to make sure everyone understands I'm joking.

Often, when I first bring out "My Little Pony" and approach Grayl, there is a twinge of anxiety as I wonder if perhaps this time she won't respond and I'll be left holding the horse. What would I do then? But so far, she's been remarkably cooperative, taking her cues from me, and thus providing some comic relief as well as demonstrating her responsiveness. The altered behaviour, from a relaxed owl sitting upright, to one with fixed attention, staring posture and, finally, aggression, is a good lesson.

"When is her birthday?" asked a child at a school in The Pas. The question took me by surprise, but I glibly replied that it was May 6. Then, checking my watch, I added: "Why, that's today!" Astonishingly, the kids at once all began to sing "Happy Birthday," an exuberant chorus that seemed based on an urge to communicate their affection for the bird. At another school that day, and again a few days later at a Flin Flon school, I deliberately mentioned the owl's supposed birthday – well, she hatched sometime in May – thus encouraging further singing. This is a ruse I'll have to be careful not to use on the same children some year in the wrong month. Is this educational? Probably not, but at the time it happened, it seemed useful, a good way to let off some steam, and a way of promoting a pleasant feeling toward the owl. And, hopefully, toward owls in general.

A Nervous Moment

Letting the owl fly over the audience is now a regular feature of school tours, but this aspect developed slowly. I had become aware that when I brought the owl near her perch, whether in a shopping mall or school gymnasium, she had an urge to get on it in a hurry. The perch came to represent security, a familiar item in an unfamiliar situation, and she was able to spot the perch from a distance. Once she saw the perch, she would attempt to fly to it; I had to restrain her by holding the tether. I learned to divert her attention as we approached the perch, then let her fly the last few yards, running up to allow her to get onto the perch. Eventually, I let her fly across an empty gym to her perch, a few flaps and a long glide which she seemed to enjoy. And finally, I let her fly with people present. At first, I let an assistant take the owl to the opposite side of the gym, behind the audience, while I stood beside the perch. I thought I could direct the owl's attention to the perch, and I wanted to be there to hook her back up to the perch. It soon became clear, however, that Grayl could identify the perch without me, and I came to realize that once she landed on the perch she'd stay there. Now, after telling the audience what to expect, and pointing out that the owl will fly only once, I do it all by myself.

Grayl on her way.

Each time the bird flies free over the heads of children or a mixed audience of young and old, I feel a certain apprehension. On a few occasions she has landed somewhere other than on the perch, including up in the rafters in a large gym. At one school, I gave my whole presentation with Grayl perched high above us on the rafters. After such an experience at one school, a young student wrote to me as follows: "Don't feel bad or embarrassed because...Lady Grayl flew way up to the wall or roof...I am very, very glad that Lady Grayl didn't get hurt." So was I. Getting the owl to come back down is a problem. It has usually involved tossing the glove or an eraser up at her until, in annoyance, she flies down to where I can reach her. But I've gained confidence and trust as the owl repeatedly goes straight to her perch. The owl develops confidence as well. She knows her perch and, despite a room full of people, strikes off spiritedly, giving three or four deep flaps of those immense wings, then gliding low over the heads of her audience and back up onto the perch. The kids yell! Just before landing, Grayl drops down almost to floor level, then, having reduced her forward momentum to zero, she swoops up onto the perch, at once turning around to face her audience. She even seems to enjoy the bedlam of excited kids (and parents and teachers) overwhelmed by the sight of this large raptor passing overhead.

Letting the owl fly to her perch over the heads of children in a gym is one thing, letting her fly over an audience in a dark movie theatre is quite another. But that's what we did for a public lecture in the Roxy Theatre one night at Neepawa. The theatre was dark, but the stage lights were on and Grayl's perch stood out in the centre of the stage. I had carefully explained to the audience just what I was proposing to do, then I walked up the aisle with Grayl to the back of the theatre. I was more than a little nervous, but I reasoned that the sight of her familiar perch would provide a suitable target. I pointed her toward the distant perch, then, when I sensed that she was focused on it, unsnapped her tether. Her performance, silent flight low over the heads, dropping lower, almost disappearing over the front rows, then swooping up onto her perch and immediately turning around to face the crowd, drew a great round of applause.

Pellets for Kids

For about a dollar each, teachers can buy owl pellets from commercial sources. These dried, regurgitated balls of indigestible fur, feathers and bones are the remains of prey ingested, in this case, by barn owls. Collected by enterprising people from roosts and nest-sites, the pellets provide information on the food habits of these birds. For school children, dissecting pellets offers a unique learning experience. Like archaeologists, boys and girls pick apart pellets, separating feathers and fur from bones. Even the youngest kids can explore these titbits from the owl's world, discovering skulls, jaw bones, skeletal parts of all kinds. The sometimes elaborate classroom reconstructions of mouse skeletons mounted on cardboard sheets that I've been shown show the amount of interest generated by this exercise.

Grayl has contributed in a limited way to this activity. I collect pellets from her pen almost daily, placing them on a shelf to dry in the sun. (A pellet is usually cast about twelve hours after ingesting food.) Grayl watches me closely as I search the pen, looking for the latest pellet, an object not always easy to see against the gravel floor of the pen. When I pick one up, flicking off bits of gravel, she pays close attention. It's easier to see pellets in winter, though some get covered by snow and show up only in spring. Often, I need to pry a pellet loose from where it has fallen, for they come out hot enough to melt the snow. It makes me aware of that hot interior where mice are digested. Later, I set them indoors for further drying, then, when there are enough on hand, I put them in plastic bags which are packed away for safekeeping.

There are not enough pellets available from this source to supply all the schools that are interested in this program. After all, Grayl produces only one or two pellets per day, but nearly all the pellets from this bird are given without charge to classes studying owls. It's one more way in which we are encouraging an interest in birds of prey. Of course, pellets from Grayl contain only the remains of laboratory mice (and occasionally small rats), so there is not the variety of species found in the pellets from wild barn owls. Grayl's pellets vary in colour – white, brown, black, gray – depending on the colours of the mice she's eaten.

Compared to wild mice, lab mice are relatively sparsely furred, hence Grayl's pellets are generally much smaller than pellets collected from wild great gray owls. Pellets from owls feeding on meadow voles, especially, are massive by comparison. The large amount of fur on those choice food items results in a felt-like bulk that surrounds and encloses the bones. Grayl's small pellets often have skeletal parts protruding, an aspect that sometimes worries me. A sharp leg bone sticking out from a pellet looks difficult to cough up, if not dangerous. The mucus coating, however, seems to provide protection, and of course the large gape of the owl allows for expulsion of fairly large pellets. Students often ask about the location and size of her mouth, a feature not easily described. Only when she is regurgitating a pellet or during an occasional yawn is there a chance to see the open mouth. One day (April 22, 1986), I found a pellet in Grayl's pen with a large wood chip attached. It was 38 mm long, 25 mm wide and 3 mm thick. Encased with mouse hair and a few fine bones, it had clearly been swallowed and regurgitated. I couldn't see how something that large could have been ingested accidentally. Still, no harm was done.

In an intriguing book about the northern harrier (formerly marsh hawk), Wisconsin raptor enthusiast Frances Hamerstrom states: "A bird that is about to cough up a pellet is almost never in a mood to eat or hunt." In fact, it appears that the sight of a mouse may even stimulate the regurgitation process. One late afternoon in July, immediately after I showed Grayl a dead mouse, she gaped widely four times, as if about to cast a pellet, but nothing came out. A few minutes later, however, in my absence she did cast a pellet. On another day, in the evening when I normally feed her, she refused a mouse. She merely raised her lower eyelids slightly, which gave her a rather musing expression, so I left five small mice for her. When I returned thirty minutes later, there was a fresh pellet on the snow and all five mice had been eaten. One winter when Herb Copland, my owl-catching companion, was trying to lure an owl to his net with a live mouse, something similar happened. The owl was perched on a fence-post beside the road, watching the mouse with considerable interest but unwilling to come for it. This went on for a fairly long time, but since the owl stayed there I encouraged Herb to keep trying. Herb remained kneeling in the snow, keeping the mouse in motion, trying to tempt the owl. Several minutes later, the owl cast a pellet, and then immediately flew to get the mouse which it had never taken its eyes off. Herb netted it as skillfully as ever.

Occasionally, when we're in the middle of a presentation, especially in mid-afternoon, Grayl will cast a pellet. Since there are distinctive signs signalling this event, I've sometimes been able to direct everyone's attention to what is happening. "Watch her, she's about to cough up a pellet," I predict. A few times I've been wrong, but generally it happens. Grayl leans forward, face downward, concentrating, slowly shaking her head from side to side, a curious sight. Then she opens her bill wide, still wagging her head, and expels a pellet which is covered with mucus to expedite a smooth ejection. Sometimes, by holding my cupped hand below her face, I am able to catch the pellet, receiving the hot slippery bolus with ease. The mucus coating imparts a silvery sheen to a freshly-dried pellet, an effect soon lost if the pellet is rained upon.

Following the worthy example provided by Fran

Hamerstrom, who experimentally tasted food regurgitated by a golden eagle, I have tentatively tasted a few fresh pellets. The mucus layer is rather sweet, but the interior mass is bitter and unpleasant. When Grayl cast a pellet at a girls' school (Balmoral Hall), one brave student volunteered to taste it, and so she did, while her classmates cheered. Then the teacher ran to get a camera, and had her do it a second time. Then three more girls wanted a lick of the still warm pellet. All this while, one girl kept saying she didn't think it was such a good idea.

Analysis of pellets collected in the field provides important information on raptor food habits. Because owls often swallow their prey whole, identification of prey species, and relative numbers taken, is possible. It is a valuable and fundamental exercise. For the great gray owl in this region, one species of mammal comprises the primary food source. The meadow vole makes up 84 percent of its diet. Thus, the reproductive fortunes of great gray owls depend strikingly on the ups and downs of this naturally cyclic species. To understand the great gray owl, one must strive to know their interrelationships with the small creatures of forest and bog.

Questions and Answers

A question often asked by school children at a presentation is, "When does she sleep?" It's generally assumed that owls are active at night and, hence, must sleep in the daytime. This is true of many, although some kinds of owls do the opposite. In general, owls tend to be crepuscular. This means that they're most active in the early hours before dawn and in late evening, as are mice and voles. Yet here is an owl that at times is on stage all day long. So, when does she sleep? At times during a school visit, or in a shopping mall, she does doze off, despite any amount of noisy distractions, even a gym full of kids. She's so used to this routine that when she tires, she simply lets go, relaxes, withdraws, bringing her greyish-white lower eyelids up until, just that fast, she is gone. Just before her eyes close, her pupils get very big. At times, I may even have to nudge her, or tap her toes, to get her to open her eyes. So she catnaps, catching a wink when she can. Of course, she sleeps when she needs to, both at night and in the daytime.

When she's sleeping in cold weather, she's fluffed out, sitting low on her perch, the upper part of the facial disk brought forward so that the eyes appear sunken. Usually, the bill is concealed by overlapping feathers. On a bright warm day at noon, I often see her on a perch, sort of folded in, head bowed a bit, eyes closed, resting if not sleeping. Either way, I've never found her sleeping so deeply that the least little sound of significance wouldn't awaken her.

This is undoubtedly characteristic of owls. Watching wild great gray owls, we learn that a female incubating eggs or brooding young often dozes off, closing her eyes and remaining still. When the male is not hunting, he may sit perched against the trunk of a tree for long periods, eyes closed, resting, apparently asleep. But it's not a real sleep, the bird is pretty much on full alert even with its eyes closed. Of course, this has survival value. When is an owl safe? When can an owl afford to ignore all sights and, especially, sounds? We don't really know much about the habits of owls at night. This is a difficult aspect to study. Despite all the years we've spent studying wild great gray owls, their nighttime behaviour largely escapes our attention. It's an area of fruitful, though difficult, research.

"Does she recognize you?" Yes, sure she does. Why should she not? Birds in general show a high level of individual recognition, from chickens in a hen-house to a family group of chickadees. This doesn't necessarily imply much intelligence, but it does indicate that birds are perceptive, quick to learn, and have good memories. When I enter Grayl's pen, or even get close to the pen, she invariably greets me with a subdued call. Neither my wife nor I ever get the excited reaction Grayl shows to strangers. Persons approaching her pen for the first time are likely to elicit an aggressive, challenging response, in which the owl hoots loudly and, if the newcomer comes closer, claws forcefully at the wire screen. Her attack – and when she flies fast across the pen to slam her feet against the screen, it clearly is an attack – is so aggressive, that I warn people not to get too close. Naturally, her response varies with her mood; at times she simply stays well back in her pen, not so much sulking, as being unwilling to move off a perch where she's been dozing.

Another question that often arises is, "Is she affectionate?" I usually gloss over that one, preferring to emphasize the "she's not a pet" aspect. In truth, she can be affectionate, though it's not something that's readily obvious, and I can't demonstrate it. In her pen, she often responds to me by giving a low soft call, a kind of plaintive murmur or soft humming. I take this as a special greeting, a sign of recognition, if not affection, for she doesn't seem to give this to others. Sometimes I can elicit it. To get an impression of this barely discernible call, say "hoo" softly, in the back of the throat, with lips almost completely closed.

At other times, I may hear this call given more forcefully, from a considerable distance. There is a surprising variability in quality of intonation: "Hoo-ooh, Hoo-ooh-ooh," conveying a wide range of feeling, as I perceive it. It is a subtle melody, differing from the challenging hooting of aggression only in its strength and emotional content. As she vocalizes, her breath is warm on my fingers held up to her bill. And she opens her bill to vocalize, something that is not readily apparent because of the feathers that surround the bill. There are also soft melodious murmurings, chirring, chirping sounds, and other subdued expressions. So pairs of wild owls at their nests must communicate with each other delicately and discretely.

In the pen, she readily hops onto my right shoulder, then at once turns around so that we're both facing the same direction. With her on my shoulder, I can walk around, pick up pellets, even spin rapidly without dislodging her. She'll sit there for up to five minutes, perfectly at ease, then suddenly fly off to a perch. When I've carried her on the glove in a large crowd, say in a mall, she has occasionally shown an urge to get up onto my shoulder, as if for security at that height or in that position. I don't like that as an image in public, so I've always avoided that situation.

Grayl also exhibits affection by reaching out and bunting my knuckles with her closed bill or by gently nibbling on my hand. I enjoy the sense of reassurance that this gives me, and usually before I leave the pen, after any casual visit, I offer her my closed hand just for the pleasure of receiving her little gesture of friendship.

Twice, school-children have asked me what I will do with Grayl when she dies. It's something I'd never thought of. "Cry a lot," I answered the first time, but the real answer eludes me. Have her body mounted? Enshrined? A proper burial? A museum specimen? Well, that time may be a long way off. An earlier decision may have to be made regarding someone to look after her when I'm no longer able. Our oldest record of a great gray owl in the wild, so far, is thirteen years, but in captivity they've been known to live more than twice as long. Suppose she lives another twenty years – I'd be ninety!

Sometimes, I get asked how long I've been studying owls, or if I've studied other kinds of birds. I like the topic, for it gives me a chance to talk about careers in wildlife or ornithology. And I don't mind pointing out that, one way or another, I've been paid most of my working life to study birds. I enjoy advising young people to sharpen their communication skills, emphasizing that it's still important to become adept at reading, writing and speaking. I like to think that there is value in having a retired civil servant give some inkling of his career and personal life. And the kids seem to enjoy it.

Once, a classroom discussion led to my telling the kids how I'd had a nervous breakdown, not exactly bird of prey material, but related. This discussion was in a grade-five class at Winkler Elementary School. We'd been talking about how calm Grayl appeared in the midst of all the confusion, and a question was asked about her seeming indifference to noise. I attempted to explain that the owl's brain was able to effectively screen out unimportant sounds, allowing the bird to concentrate, or respond, to sounds of significance. This would explain why I can shout or even blow a whistle next to Grayl without upsetting her, or even causing her to blink. There is a damping effect, I suggested, a function of the brain that keeps us all from being over-stimulated, that keeps us sane. I went on from there – with all the kids listening attentively and quietly – to describe how during a severe emotional upset I had often experienced the lack of the usual screening or damping effect. As a result, I explained, an unexpected sound, such as a car back-firing, or even a spoon dropped on a plate, would shock me. It seems, I continued, that some things work much the same way for both owls and people.

No End In Sight

Grayl and I have now visited more than a hundred elementary schools. At an average of two hundred students, that's perhaps twenty thousand students who have been exposed to the program and to this tireless bird. We have visited schools in forty-five cities and towns outside of Winnipeg. We've driven north to Flin Flon, Thompson and Gillam, and east to Dryden, visiting schools and giving public presentations. We've even been to southern Wisconsin and Minnesota. Our visits to schools in Kenora and Dryden were made in response to requests from the Ontario Ministry of Natural Resources, which provided financial and logistical support for our owl research. In the same way, we gave a seminar in St. Paul because of support received from the U.S. Forest Service. Wherever we've been, the response to the bird has been warm and enthusiastic. It was thrilling to pull into the parking lot at the Flin Flon School to be surrounded immediately by a host of children shouting gleefully: "It's the owl! It's Grayl!"

A visit to a school usually lasts for an hour or two, but occasionally I have stayed for up to six hours. A trip to a rural school invariably takes a whole day, or may necessitate staying overnight. I try to keep a flexible schedule, taking time to meet people's needs, especially where there has been an unusual effort by teachers and students to get us to come. Following a school visit, I often get letters, mostly commenting on Lady Grayl. Teachers at one school wrote to tell me that on the day following my visit, several people coming into the staff room commented on the noticeable absence of Grayl, "that sociable owl," perched on the back of a chair. I especially liked this one, sent unsigned: "I was impressed by the calmness of the owl – she sat there in complete control of herself. She definitely had a personality. I thought at times she was like a cat in some ways, in her facial features and colour. I was impressed by the fact that she was no pet, however tame and civilized she was. There had obviously been no attempt to turn her into a substitute dog or cat – no tricks."

Ardythe McMaster, grade-five teacher at Grosvenor School in Winnipeg, sent me several letters after a visit, noting: "Please accept these letters in the spirit in which they were written. They come to you fresh, happy, enthusiastic and un-edited...wide-ranging ability levels, from Leslie, who writes poetry, to Anthony, who has cerebral palsy. Everyone knows that kids enter school with vastly different abilities and backgrounds, but some people forget that they come out of school that way too!" What follows is a portion of a letter from Nina, who according to Ardythe, "is a little girl from Sweden – first year in Canada!"

> Dear Dr. Bob Nero,
> I want to thank you for coming to our school and showing us your Lady Grayl. I think she had a personal look and she was so beutiful. I have never hade a bird of any kind, but I think, that if I could I would want to have a Great

Gray Owl. (Of corse this is inposibul but you can always dream.) I don't know what I liket most about Lady Grayl? but I guess it was her personality. I think thht it was funny the way she desided to take a walk. It was almost hard to belive that the head was so small and when we were allowed to pat her, I could almost not fel her soft feathers. I also whant to thank you for giving us the owl pellets. It was really fun to take them apart and look at all the small bones in the mous body. I think that it is incredibul that the owls stomac can seperate the bones and fur from everything else. When we first got one I thot it would be a little bit slimy but it was not slimy at all. I was lucky enough to get a owl pellet with a prity good scall in it. After we found almost all the bones we put them on a piece of paper and made a little display in our classroom and the younger kids came to look at them. It was great fun. And now about the pictures in the hall that you saw. They were realy fun to make, first we colored the paper in owly-colors and then we put temper paint over that and then we scratched it out, and when we're finished, you could look at the real owl and see what the differnts was, and there was a lot of differents and I must say that I liket the real owl better.

Thanks ones agian for coming.

Your truly, Nina.

At one small rural community, after a presentation to an audience including parents and general public, I took Grayl into a grade-three classroom for a special session. A lad sitting at the front was surprised when I let Grayl jump down off the glove onto his desk. While the rest of the class laughed, the boy sat back, rigid with alarm. Later, Chris Budd wrote to me as follows: "Dear Dr. Nero, I got a good look at her and my shoes were falling off. I hope I can see her again on my desk. I didn't wash my desk." A few times, letters I've received have moved me to reply. What follows is the letter I sent to Chris' class on behalf of the owl:

Message from Lady Grayl
November 21, 1991
Dear Owl Kids:

Thanks for all the kind words about my performance at your school...Dr. Bob showed me all the letters and drawings...I'm not too good at reading, but I can appreciate the pictures. Nice going! You guys really know what owls look like. We didn't have any problems getting back to Winnipeg (where we live) that day after we left St. Alphonse, although when we got down in the flat country there was some blowing snow...we followed a big truck for a long time, most of the way back to the big city. Not too much to see on the way, oh, a few Snow Buntings, mostly blowing snow, car headlights coming and going...and finally there we were back on familiar ground, turning into our driveway...and there was my house in Dr. Bob's backyard...it gives me a warm feeling when he takes me out of the car, holds me up high on his glove so I can spread my wings, and then he runs all the way to the back of the yard...this lets me cool off, and then I'm in my neat flightpen, turned loose, up onto the highest perch, back home again!

I forgot to tell you that those were MY pellets you dissected. Glad to donate them. Of course, they contained only laboratory mouse remains, the only food Dr. Bob lets me have...some day I'd like to try something exotic, say, liver and onions! (I'm only kidding, those mice really contain all the nutrients I need to keep healthy and in good shape). Some of the pellets are grey, brown, white or black...it depends on the colour of the mouse, and they come in different colours. Dr. Bob comes into my house every day to pick up pellets...I'm coughing them up (he'd rather I said "regurgitating") once a day, sometimes twice. He looks for them in the snow on the floor of my house, puts them in a row on a shelf outside the pen, then collects them once a week or so, taking them in his house to dry out. What a guy...for a long time I didn't know what he was doing with them, and I sure *wondered. I thought maybe he was just trying to tidy up the floor for me. It is weird the way he grunts whenever he bends down to pick up a pellet, I guess his back hurts a little, and it's sort of fun to watch the way he picks off the little stones, though now there's enough snow over the floor of most of my house so he doesn't have to worry about that. I like the snow, it feels great on my feet, and when I walk in it I leave these neat tracks. Winter is a great time, as long as I get enough to eat.*

Boy, you guys sure ask a lot of questions, but I guess that when you're in school that is the time to find out about things, and you never know when a piece of information is going to come in handy. Such as where are the ears on an owl...I never thought about that. Do you think about your ears? Mostly, I just sit around and listen...oh, I don't pay much attention to things that don't interest me, jets overhead, city traffic (we live near a busy thoroughfare), doors slamming etc. I tend to concentrate on the sounds of movement in the leaves on the ground, a bird passing by, things that you guys would never think much about, and some things you wouldn't even be able to hear. When I'm in a group of kids at a school I feel pretty good, so I relax, and I don't hardly mind when Dr. Bob insists on lifting my face feathers and showing people my ears, such as they are, though it tickles a little sometimes.

Perhaps the funniest thing about this weird relationship I have with Dr. Bob is the way he reacts when I huff and puff and give a toy animal the beady-eyed look...boy, sometimes he gets serious and even writes things down in a little notebook. Oh, he pretends that he's looking the other way, but I've noticed that whenever I fluff up a little or stare hard at a passing hawk (those birds bother me a lot for some reason, there is something I don't like about the way they look, that great hooked beak? something hard to define) then right away he's taking notes on my BEHAVIOUR...heck, I can't do anything without having him peering at me from under-

neath those shaggy grey eyebrows and nervously twitching his mouth. Oh, he's O.K., but if he knew all the things I do when he's not here to record my behaviour, he'd be astonished. He thinks he knows something about owls, well, sure he knows more than most people, but there is still a lot, I mean a whole lot, for him to learn. And there are some things he never will understand about me and my kind.

And thanks for the poems. Dr. Bob does a fair job with the poetry but the two poems from your school were just terrific.

We've been to three schools in Winnipeg since we were at your school. That makes about 38 different schools altogether since we started doing this project. He, Dr. Bob, that is, would write to each of you kids, but boy, that's a lot of kids, about 3000 just in the past 3 months. It was a treat meeting you, and maybe we'll get together again. So keep smiling and, remember, GIVE A HOOT!

Much love, Lady Grayl

People with cameras naturally focus on Lady Grayl, but I keep wanting to tell them to photograph the kids, all those beaming faces watching the owl, following her every movement. How different is my view of a presentation, for I'm at the front watching them. And how satisfying and emotionally arousing this is. As the owl-man, I'm much in the centre of things, from the moment I arrive at a school until I drive away. It can be exhilarating. Excited, keyed-up, anxious, I'm prone to seek comfort in drawing near to almost every person, especially my contacts, the person or persons involved in arranging for the visit. I imagine that some people find me overly forward, but I reach for the principal's, or teacher's hand, male or female, as if for security.

I use my role as the owl-man to reach across the years and social barriers. In a way, I take advantage of the situation, seeking to solicit kind words, affection, reassurance, drawing upon the generosity of nearly everyone I meet. I use the owl; hardly anyone can resist her spell. She has an effect on people. I see it over and over again when Lady Grayl is brought into a room on the glove, people are totally charmed by her beauty and calm demeanour. She is my ruse, my "open sesame."

Touching the owl remains a privilege extended to certain individuals or groups. On May 21, 1993, for example, at our first visit to a Hutterite Brethren school, interest in owl matters was so high that I invited everyone to come forward, one at a time, to touch the owl. The value of this exercise may be judged by a poem written later by a grade-four student:

Lady Grayl

Her feathers are soft
like thickest
homemade feather quilt
my fingertips disappear in her
thick feathers.
The owl spreads out its wings
soundlessly flies away from
staring children.

- Alyson Maendel, Fairholme Colony

CHAPTER 5

A Fall of Feathers

UNDER GRAYL'S SCRUTINY, FROM LATE APRIL THROUGH AUGUST I invade her sanctum daily to retrieve moulted feathers – a curious task. It is one of the reasons I haven't had any summer holidays for several years. The aim is to record the fall of feathers, this annual shedding of the old and growth of the new, whereby birds renew their plumage. It happens once a year in most birds, and twice a year in a few species such as the bobolink. In the latter species there is even a colour change from one moult to the next. In adult owls, there is only one moult each year and no change in colour. The new feathers are always the same colour, but they are easy to tell from the old because those feathers have faded. This is especially noticeable in wild owls. Females that may have spent long hours sitting on a nest exposed to sunlight are strikingly faded. But even Grayl, with limited exposure to direct sunlight, shows this effect, though to a lesser degree.

We had observed in wild great gray owls that the moult of the flight feathers, those great pinions that carry these birds through the air, was incomplete. This means that after the finish of moult in fall, and over winter, there were always some old flight feathers along with the new. They were easy to tell apart, for the new ones were glossy dark grey, the old sun-faded and worn to a dull brown. We reasoned that this strange feature, which varied considerably between individuals, was probably affected by energy demands during the breeding season, and perhaps by availability of prey. Thus, it was of considerable interest to see what would happen in the tame owl.

Grayl has little to do during the moult period. Usually I reduce our outings in summer, partly because school is out, but also because she starts looking pretty ragged, and she is sometimes cranky. Besides, at that time she's dropping feathers and I might miss an important one. The number of loose feathers in the pen on some days is surprising to those who haven't followed a moult period in a large bird. House sparrows, abundant in our yard because of our feeders and a risky nesting opportunity in our neighbour's purple martin house, sometimes invade Grayl's pen to retrieve a few to feather their nest. When our friends clean the sparrow nests out of the martin house they often find a large number of Grayl's feathers. And the red squirrel that lives beneath the brush pile – well, it lives all over the place, running freely through the trees – also gathers feathers for its hidden winter nest.

All these years, by visiting Grayl's pen daily, I have recorded the date on which each flight feather fell. It was useful to discover that she also shows an incomplete moult of flight feathers in every season, despite having food available daily throughout the year. Just as in wild great gray owls, some primaries and secondaries are retained for two years before being shed. This proves that there is a basic pattern of incomplete moult of the major wing feathers in this species. (The variations within that pattern and the timing of the moult of individual feathers, as well as the pattern of moult over the entire body, are aspects that I am still recording and analyzing.)

The moult of wing feathers is a gradual process, occurring over the summer, and at no time is Grayl unable to fly. There are always enough feathers present to allow for flight. This is true of most birds, although the waterfowl – ducks, geese and swans – are exceptional, remaining flightless for a few weeks owing to a nearly simultaneous moult.

Annually in mid-June, Grayl sheds her entire tail over a period of two weeks or less. The short tail means she has to work a little harder to maintain her balance on landing. Grayl's

A *detailed look*.

A *little ragged*.

new tail feathers grow to full length in about two months. Presumably, wild birds moult their tail feathers in the same way, and it must be more of a problem for them. Tail moult occurred in one wild nesting female great gray owl at a much earlier time, beginning even before she laid the first egg. I found the first feather on the ground on April 2, 1977, beneath one of the nests we made. By May 8, she had completed the tail moult, shedding all but the central two feathers which were retained.

Grayl's first set of rectrices or tail feathers, her juvenile set, were a little narrower and slightly shorter than the adult set obtained in her first moult and thereafter. This is generally the case for raptors.

As mentioned in my 1980 book, a tail feather from a great gray owl provides a lesson in beauty and adaptability. More than 30 cm long and 6 cm wide, it is a reminder of the large tail of this relatively small-bodied bird. The feather's light weight is impressive: despite its size, it floats to the floor when dropped, and it lifts with the slightest breath. Considering the function of the tail, an individual feather is remarkably soft and flexible. Mottled greyish brown, with alternating light and dark bars, it appears denser than it is. When pressed against a printed page the letters show through clearly, even through the darkest parts, and the grayish-white bars and spots seem almost nonexistent. The central two tail feathers, which are longer and usually greyer (or brown, if faded) than the others, are nearly transparent. Coloured objects are visible through the vanes even when held 20 cm away.

It was intriguing to discover that the timing of moult of individual feathers was highly regulated. For example, in four successive years, Grayl's twelve tail feathers were shed between June 3 and June 29. Her tail moult is not synchronous, that is, the twelve main feathers or rectrices don't fall out all at the same time. Instead, they are shed one or two every day or so over a period of about two weeks, as follows: June 3-13,

June 10-21, June 12-24, June 9-29. A few rectrices fell with surprising calendar regularity from year to year. Number three left, for example, fell on June 18 (1990), 18 ('91) and 16 ('92); number three right fell on June 14 ('90), 15 ('91) and 14 ('92). Considering the possible error in finding a feather on the floor of Grayl's pen in the morning that may have fallen the previous night before midnight, this is highly regular. Another example: primary number ten, the outermost flight feather on the left wing, was dropped on July 24 in 1986 and 1988, on July 23 in 1990, and on July 27 in 1992, being retained for the years in between those dates.

I find the regularity astonishing. Moult must be initiated by day length, a factor that influences many biological events. No other natural force has such regularity. Thus, the timing of the fall of feathers, genetically established in each species, is set in motion through the effect of exposure to changing periods of lightness and darkness. I can understand this, but what keeps individual feathers on time? Why should one particular primary feather fall before another? And what directs the retention of one feather and not the adjacent one? Is there built in programming in the feather follicle where growth of a new feather begins? And how and why does nutritional level affect the process? I'm way over my head here, but clearly here is yet another area for further investigation.

Only a proportion of her flight feathers are replaced in any one season. In 1992, for example, only half of the secondaries, and twelve out of twenty primaries were shed. If a flight feather is damaged accidentally, it must remain as it is for another season before being renewed, unless it is prescribed to be moulted that year. Moult proceeds without concern for such irregularities, following a strategic course evolved over the ages to provide effective rejuvenation of feathers.

But accidents do happen. One year, when Grayl suffered a broken tail feather in April, I repaired it by attaching an appropriate length cut from a feather in the same position, one shed in a previous year. In a process called "imping," a term borrowed from falconry, a round piece of wood pointed at both ends and coated with glue is thrust into the hollow quill of each feather, allowing them to be joined. Falconers keep a supply of feathers on hand, using them to repair the broken

Something's missing.

pinions of birds they fly, thus keeping them in top form. This year, Grayl has a primary feather that is split for some distance on the end. I have no idea how it happened, and I was hoping that it would be moulted, but it wasn't in the schedule. It will have to stay the way it is until next year's moult, for I'm reluctant to try to imp on such a large feather. Besides, there's the

"I'm moulting, OK?"

problem of subjecting Grayl to such a trying procedure. Maybe no one will notice the damaged feather.

Occasionally, a moulting feather, loosened by the growth of the replacement, will be bitten and tugged at by Grayl, suggesting that there is some slight irritation connected with this process. On June 4, 1987, at midnight, I watched her bite and then pull out a tail feather; she toyed with it, then unceremoniously dropped it. This business of moult can be messy. Hundreds of new feathers grow, each one forcing out the old. The new feather is fat at the base, a blood-filled quill that gradually splits, exposing the emerging feather vanes. Grayl sometimes scratches vigorously, not unlike a house cat, raking herself with a long talon, especially around the face.

I've learned that she doesn't mind having me gently massage her closed eyes, at least during the period of moult. Doubtless, new feathers emerging on the eyelids can at times itch, and this may be an area where she's not likely to scratch with her talons. When I do this, pressing down fairly firmly on her eyeballs, there is little of the submissive lowering of her head (withdrawal?) as when she is being patted on the head by people who want to pet her as one would a cat or dog. Rather, she remains upright, apparently enjoying the sensation of having me rub her eyes. She lets me press down hard enough so that I can feel the liquid resiliency of her eyeballs; it is a weird sensation.

Of the two toes on each foot that we see on a perched owl, it is the outer one that is used in scratching. This is actually the centre toe of the typical three-toes-forward bird foot. In owls, the outermost toe is reversible, and is almost always directed backwards. Thus, owls have two grasping toes in front and two behind. When we see tracks in the snow, however, we note that the outermost toe points to the side. A knife-like ridge that runs the length of the talon of the central toe increases its effectiveness in scratching or in scraping the bill. It is a feature of many owls, if not all, and numerous other birds. In the barn owl, this ridge is serrated, but no one knows why.

Vigorous scratching of her face during moult loosens feathers and a snowstorm of white fragments of quill debris. It's another reason for wanting to let her rest in her pen at this time of the year. When I see a feather sticking out of her plumage at an angle, clearly ready to fall, I've been tempted more than once to reach out to dislodge it or pull it away. But the gesture of my hand towards her usually brings a sharp nip

"Don't laugh."

and a hard glare. On June 8, 1993, when I pulled lightly on a loose tail feather, she glowered at me. Then, when I gestured toward my right shoulder, instead of simply landing there as she often does, she struck hard enough to give me several scratches through my shirt. It was the first aggressive encounter of the year. "Leave me be, leave it alone," she seems to imply, and so I mostly do.

By mid-August, much of Grayl's plumage has been shed and replaced. Only the feathers of her crown and nape still look faded and unkempt, tufts of brown feathers sticking up above the new emerging layer of plumes. Glossy, dark and perfect in their newness, they contrast strikingly with the older brown ones, still to fall. As I stand and admire the effect, it strikes me that what I'm seeing is the development of the winter coat – feathers that will give this bird the necessary protection on cold dark nights in January. Here, in late summer, she is readying herself for winter. All these feathers falling and renewing are but preparation for the cold months, that time that tests the survival ability of all residents of these northern climes. With temperatures falling at times to forty below zero and lower, with fierce winds, with deep snow covering the owls' food supply, winter is the time for which all this plumage renewal is geared. This is when it has to work. Before the first snow falls, the owl is as well prepared for the vicissitudes of winter as any creature can be. If not actually enjoying winter – and sometimes I think Grayl does, or is certainly comfortable in it – at least she is well equipped to handle it with ease. That is, as long as she gets her two or three mice daily.

Behaviour, too, has evolved to meet their needs. So we find great gray owls seeking prey they can't see beneath the snow, plunging head downwards, face forward, into the snow, crashing even through icy crusts, at times nearly disappearing from sight. Those huge feathered heads are sound-collectors, helping them hear small mammals.

Compared to snowy owls, great gray owls have relatively loose feathering. The wind ruffles the light feathers of the flanks, breast and back of the head, occasionally even tilting the long tail. But the relatively stiff feathering of the face remains intact, unmoved even by a strong wind.

The most impressive aspect of the body feathers I retrieve is their buoyancy, their downiness, features that provide the insulation that holds the owl's warmth against the body. Nearly all the body feathers are of this nature, but the long feathers of the undertail coverts, the lower breast and the flanks are especially remarkable in this respect. These are the feathers I often send to people as tokens of appreciation. Sometimes the response is surprising. Terry Lind, Edmonton, sent a cheque for $25, adding, "The information you provided in your recent correspondence with my father, Frank Lind of Bluffton, Alberta, has been most valuable. On a more personal note, allow me to pass on my father's appreciation of the time you took to personally respond to his letter and to include a Grayl feather. Your unexpected reply has brought pleasure and encouragement to a dedicated albeit amateur naturalist." It pleases me to think of all those plumes fastened to bulletin boards, headboards, over desks – a touch of gray owl in far places.

In The Great Gray Owl: Phantom of the Northern Forest, I wrote that these feathers "may be more than nine inches long. They are highly filamentous for most of their length, bearing long, downy plumes except for the distal inch or two. Though the filaments or plumes arise laterally from the feather shaft, as do the vanes, they are extremely light and airy, floating off in all directions as if repelled electrically, giving the feather a cylindrical form. They move freely, responding instantly to the least movement of air, trembling and swinging about like the feathery appendages of some sea animal."

Worn Feathers

One surprising aspect of the moult in wild owls is that sometimes they retain old worn feathers on the head, feathers that would seem to be essential to winter survival. Nothing like this has been observed in Grayl. One can understand that a few faded and worn flight feathers could still function adequately, but occasionally we have captured birds that had badly worn plumage on the crown or front top of the head. It gave a kind of grizzled effect, looking almost as if the feathers had been singed, apparently the result of extreme wear. Abrasion, perhaps due in part to a bird plunging into snow for prey, may have been a factor. After all, such feathers would have been grown in August two years back. They would, in fact, be going through their second winter! Mid-winter moult can be found to some extent in some individuals, but summer is the chief time of moult for most birds. Evidently, lack of adequate nutrition is the cause of inhibition of moult.

In Grayl's case, the incomplete moult of flight feathers that occurs regularly must be a basic feature of the species, for she surely needs no further food. If birds are having a hard time during winter, and we know that sometimes, owing to a vole crash, this is the case, then they would save energy by growing fewer feathers.

One might expect Grayl to eat more during the moult, to provide extra nutrients for the growing feathers. Actually, she eats less in summer than in winter. At the end of the moult period, in late August, however, she begins to eat more, practically doubling her intake. Of course, new feathers continue to grow right through September. Even after she appears to have reached a final stage of feather renewal, say, in mid-September to early October, should she shake herself or flap vigorously, some feather debris is sure to fall out.

For three years, I attempted to pick up every single feather that fell, putting each day's collection into a dated envelope. Later, I attempted to identify, count and catalog each one. Although I have prepared more than one hundred great gray owl specimens for museums, collecting feathers from Grayl has given me new insights. In one season, the total number of feathers that I was able to retrieve, classify and count was 4642.

This may not be the complete number of feathers on her body, but it is probably close. It was a challenge to categorize feathers from all parts of the plumage, from the large pinions to tiny bristles. Gradually, I became acquainted with fifteen different kinds, including some fairly colourful ones. Short narrow feathers on the forehead and below the chin, if I can use these terms, are prettily marked with white and brown, separated by black bars. More colourful than any other feathers on this species, these are all mainly concealed by the facial disk. Why should this be? Perhaps these bright little feathers are a carry-over from a time in the great gray owl's evolutionary history when the bird possessed a more colourful plumage. With no biological disadvantage to retaining these feathers, I suspect that they have simply come along in time, more or less concealed by an evolving large facial disk.

Unlike most birds, owls have feathers with a soft upper or dorsal surface: a noticeable velvety pile covers the top of each one. The lower surfaces have the usual bare, glossy appearance. This is especially the case for all the flight feathers. When one feather slides over another, as in the process of flying, there is very little sound produced. This is one of several features helping owls to achieve relatively silent flight.

Certain feathers underneath the wings at the base of the primaries and secondaries have an especially heavy soft pile surface on their inner side. These feathers, the greater underwing coverts, cover the relatively bare quills of the primary and secondary feather bases, cushioning them as they spread and close. These peculiar feathers, specialized in shape and structure, are unlike any others on the underside of the wing. They have striking gray and white stripes, leading me to think of them as the "zebra feathers." They are among the last feathers to be shed. When I find one on the floor in Grayl's pen, I can't resist stroking the soft furry inner side while reflecting on what I've learned from this bird.

How to Tell the Sexes Apart

As far as we know, there is no difference in appearance between a male and a female great gray owl. Still, it wouldn't surprise me if one day some astute student discovered some difference in appearance, some subtle pattern that we have overlooked that distinguishes male from female. Great gray owls are a good example of reversed sexual dimorphism. In most birds, the male is the larger sex. However, in owls and other raptors, the female is the larger bird. This is especially so in this species. Great gray owls can easily be distinguished by size when the pair is together, but taken separately, the size difference is seldom obvious. Furthermore, nearly all measurements overlap. Weight varies so much, depending on a bird's condition, that this is not always a dependable measure.

Jim Duncan has worked out a formula for separating the sexes, taking into account folded-wing length (chord), tail length and foot-pad width. Grayl's measurements place her well within the adult female range. The most widely accepted theory for reversed dimorphism relates to a division of duties by the pair during the breeding season, the female sheltering and protecting the young, and the smaller and supposedly more agile male doing all the hunting for the family. Another theory points to the advantage of the male being smaller, and therefore more readily tolerated by the female during courtship. The burrowing owl is one of the species which exhibits normal sexual dimorphism.

Grayl has one minor plumage feature that is worth mentioning. In the middle of her breast there is a small clump of nearly white feathers, a touch of albinism. No one notices it, but it's of interest because her mother had a similar, though larger patch in the same place. We made note of the parent bird's white mark the day we captured her, for it was fairly conspicuous. Grayl also has a partly depigmented talon, another bit of albinism. The medial or inside half of the central talon on the right foot is gray instead of black. This slight abnormality was also observed in Grayl's two siblings – same foot, same toe – an obvious genetically-related trait.

Grayl's white bill, on the other hand, seems to be an individual trait, for both her parents, according to my field notes, had bright yellow bills. Bill colour in wild great gray owls varies individually, ranging from deep orange-yellow to olive-green and, just as in Grayl, white or ivory. Initially, Grayl's bill was slightly yellowish, but it soon lost all colour. At first I thought her pale bill might indicate a dietary deficiency, for the yellow pigment in birds is derived from carotene in their food. It occurred to me that wild voles feeding on green vegetation would contain more carotene than the lab mice we were feeding Grayl. And since vitamins are required to process carotene, for several weeks I injected her dead mice with a multivitamin solution before giving them to her. There was no discernible change. She is simply an owl with a pale bill, another puzzle. Note, too, that despite the pale bill, her eyes are a respectable bright yellow.

During the moult period there is a noticeable increase in growth of the bill and the talons. This results in a change in colour and an extension of the bill which gets a chalky appearance. About the time I think that the bill will need trimming – as is often the case for birds in captivity – this rapid growth ends; before long, Grayl will have worn her bill down to a normal shape. Thus, I have never had to trim her bill. The talons, too, get a chalky look, and the outer layer gradually breaks away, revealing a new and darker, more pointed core. This process may still be taking place as late as December, but by January the talons are usually full-length, glossy-dark and needle-sharp again. Much as I hate doing it – it feels like a desecration – about this time I usually bring Grayl indoors and, while she is perched, take the sharp tips off all eight talons with a nail-clipper. I do this as insurance against someone getting badly scratched. Grayl is fairly tolerant of this procedure, doesn't need the sharp tips, and the talons become pointed again in about two weeks; like the bill, they are more or less self-sharpening.

Sometimes, children and even grownups mistakenly refer to the "fur" on Grayl's feet. Heavily feathered right down the toes to the talons with short, dense plumes, they do appear furry. It's another adaptation for survival in a cold climate. I don't mind at all when kids ask about her furry feet; it gives me an opening to remind them of some basic differences between birds and mammals. But, even after saying that only mammals have fur or hair, one could add that birds do have some hairlike feathers. Many birds have highly specialized feathers called bristles, semibristles and filoplumes. As the names suggest, these don't look like feathers.

Bristles or semibristles are abundant on the face of an owl, especially around the eyelids and bill. On a cold frosty morning, these fine bristles collect frost from Grayl's breath, making them stand out. When Grayl's face is in profile and is backlighted by the sun, the fine tips of these hairlike structures gleam in surprising abundance. They apparently function as tactile sensors, like the whiskers of a cat.

Filoplumes are found on all birds at critical areas of the body, where they evidently act as pressure and vibration receptors, assisting in adjusting the position of the feathers. I have two filoplumes from Grayl in front of me as I write. Finer than a human hair, the longest measures 67 mm. These are not easily seen on the gravel floor of her pen, so I'm aware that I haven't kept track of all her moulted feathers.

Gesture

One at a time
the tame owl takes
three dead mice from me
reaching forward
head tipped slightly
nipping them skillfully
with the tip of her bill
swallowing them whole —
she takes a fourth one
lets it dangle
carries it to a platform
drops it in a corner
then pats it once
with her foot
as if to say
"now, stay there"
and moves away.

CHAPTER 6

Images

I'VE MENTIONED THAT GRAYL WAS "AFRAID" OF OWLS BECAUSE SHE HAD been imprinted at an early age on people. What we really mean, I suppose, is that while she is enormously tolerant of people, she shows a strong negative reaction to owls: they alarm her. This aspect of her behaviour merits further attention.

When Grayl saw herself in a mirror for the first time, she exploded with indignation and fury. It happened unexpectedly and stunned me. In the fall of 1984, when I was escorting her to many different places, I had carried her into the lobby of an apartment block to show to friends. When I came alongside a large wall mirror, the owl reacted vigorously, expanding all her plumage, hooting loudly, thrashing her wings in response to her image. Of course, the more she carried on, the stronger grew her supposed antagonist's display! I quickly moved away from the offending image, thinking that it would be useful to try to record this behaviour at another time.

A year later, a CBC-TV crew was on hand for a presentation at a school in Selkirk. I asked them if they would mind filming Grayl's reaction to a mirror so that we could have a permanent record of this behaviour. When they agreed, I hastened to search for a suitably large mirror. The school principal suggested that we use the bathroom mirror at his nearby home. After the cameraman set up his camera on a tripod facing the mirror, I brought in the owl. I wasn't sure what she would do, but I kept my free hand in front of her eyes until we were all in position. Then, voila! there she was in the mirror for the second time. She reacted almost at once and beautifully, making herself look big by erecting her plumage, hooting aggressively and glaring fiercely. She then scrambled up my arm and onto my shoulder, and then hopped onto my back, peering balefully over my head at the dreaded image. This was all recorded on professional video film. The CBC crew found it enthralling. In the end, they ran the footage, together with their coverage of the school presentation, on national television. They also gave me a copy of the film of the mirror-reaction to study; it is instructive.

The owl's behaviour in response to what she perceived as a threat is interesting in revealing aspects of great gray owl display. It reinforced our understanding of Grayl's negative reaction to owls, a sign of the depth of her imprinting on humans. It also seemed that she had limited powers of perception – after all, it was only a reflection. This notion was dispelled, however, when she looked at a mirror the third time. There was a much reduced response, and the fourth time I held her before a mirror there was practically no response. Thereafter, she sat before a mirror with no response. She had learned the difference. Since she still responds strongly to even a dead, frozen carcass of a great gray owl held in my hands, it is clear that she can differentiate between the image in a mirror and the real thing. Whether she is wise or not is a moot question, but this is good evidence that she learns quickly.

Perhaps any owl, suddenly confronted with an individual owl of the same species at close hand, would initially react similarly, especially if the second owl behaved the way Grayl's self-energizing image did. After all, owls are not all that sociable at close quarters. But Grayl has shown an objection to anything even remotely resembling an owl. It's hard to imagine an image more reduced in potency than a dead owl, or, even worse, a dried study skin with cotton batting in the eye cavities. When shown to Grayl, both such objects have sometimes, but not always, elicited strong responses. Basically, she raises all her back feathers, spreads her tail, droops her arched wings, and, with glaring eyes, hoots vigorously. Two examples from my notes provide details.

February 28, 1986, 11:30 a.m. - I showed her a dead, relaxed, great gray owl, one with closed eyes, and she reacted from about 20 m away. Hooting, feathers all raised, nearest wing held fully spread and lowered. When I moved the dead owl around the corner of the pen, she walked rapidly along her perch and gave a full display again, much as when she responded to her image in a mirror.

At 2:30 p.m. that same day when I approached her pen, she was clearly apprehensive, she went into her hunched over, back feathers raised, head bigger than usual display, with an intense look in her eyes. She remembered!

January 2, 1987, 3:15 p.m. - I approached the pen with a dead, frozen great gray owl held upright, one with closed eyes, but a bright yellow bill and good facial features. When I was about 20 m away, Grayl reacted, elevating all her feathers, "puffing herself up." At close range, she lowered her head, her pupils small and with that intense look she gets, scapulars fully erected, left wing fanned and down. When I changed position, she bolted over and switched wings, dropping the nearest wing, and giving a loud, fierce "Hoo-hoo-hoo!" Still holding the frozen owl, I entered the pen. She at once attacked, launching herself at the face of the owl, striking it with both feet with spread talons, then rushing back to her perch. I withdrew from the pen, then placed the owl close to the wire screen, whereupon Grayl attacked again, fierce and fast, clenching both feet against the screen. She was much upset.

I expected much less of a reaction the day I brought home a downy eastern screech-owl, one submitted to us for rehabilitation. When I took it into her pen, wondering if perhaps it might even arouse her maternal instincts, she went into a panic, flying back and forth and calling in alarm until it was withdrawn. Of course, her response to these things varies somewhat, apparently depending on the nature of the object, the way it is presented to her, and her own mood at the time.

Elements of Grayl's agonistic (attack-escape) display are variable and include raising all or parts of the plumage, altering body position by lowering the head, crouching or standing tall, spreading one or both wings, and vocalizing. Any or all may be used in any one situation, depending on the stimulus. Similar displays are seen in other birds. My years with red-winged blackbirds provided good experience for interpreting the behaviour of other birds, for all, it turns out, have some things in common. Owls are certainly different creatures, but after all, they're still birds. So it should be no surprise to find similarities between redwings and great gray owls. It is mainly a matter of understanding the nature of bird behaviour.

I like what Berndt Heinrich had to say on this topic, "Birds are primarily emotional beings, and their responses to emotional drives are probably much more direct than ours are, since human reactions are tempered by reason." With this in mind, consider for a moment the spread-tail display of the

"I hate young owls, dead or alive!"

redwing, whereby the tail feathers are spread and brought forward in accompaniment to typical territorial song-spread display. The spread-tail also is seen in antagonistic situations, denoting aroused aggression.

Grayl fans her tail and brings it forward in moments of arousal related to assertiveness or aggression. Once she is in this mood – slightly hunched over and bristling a little, perhaps in response to some object I'm pushing toward her – then one can see the tail spread and relax alternately as the object is thrust forward and withdrawn. This happens, to a limited extent, whenever I bring the toy horse into play to demonstrate the behaviour for school children. It is also an important component of Grayl's response to live or mounted birds of prey.

I will be the first to admit that we are a long way from understanding the meaning, that is, the use and function, of these several aspects of behaviour. Vocalizations alone will take some time and patience to unravel, for there are evidently significant attributes to subtle differences in tone and quality of so simple an expression as hooting. The range of vocalizations is broad, and I don't intend to go into this aspect here. For each particular call there are numerous variations, often subtle; one has to listen closely to get the feeling behind a vocalization. At any level there is an emotional content to a display; detecting and recording these features is probably worth another thesis. Aggressive/defensive attitudes can vary in intensity momentarily, depending again upon the stimulus source, a bird's changing mood, and other factors, including experience.

Owl Meets Owl

Grayl's first encounter with a live great gray owl took place on a wintry day, March 12, 1991, near Hecla Island, 175 km north of Winnipeg. It was a tough drive. About an hour out of

Winnipeg, we ran into blowing snow. The conditions caused a dangerous "white-out," making it difficult to see the road. After giving a presentation with Grayl at a Project WILD seminar, we

A *sense of unease, note the exposed bill.*

drove away in late afternoon with snow still falling. Shortly after leaving the causeway to the island we came upon an owl perched in a tree about 135 m off the highway. Because visibility was poor, I took Grayl out of the car on the glove and held her up high until she saw the other owl. In a minute the wild owl saw her and raised its head high for a moment, then resumed hunting. Grayl responded almost at the same time, fluffing out her feathers, hissing and bill-snapping. When I returned her to the car, she at once leaped up onto the stump, facing the distant object of her wrath, in the look-how-big-and-ferocious-I-am display, huffing and puffing, as it were, and elevating all her feathers. Her head was fully as large as a soccer ball, her wings were held out and down, and she hooted forcefully: "Woo-hoo-hooooh-hoo!" This chillingly aggressive calling reminded me of times when I had been threatened or attacked by a wild female owl at a nest.

When the wild owl flew to a closer perch, Grayl became even more excited, thrusting her chin forward belligerently. When I turned the car around so that Grayl could have a better look at the owl in its new position, she moved around in order to keep the owl in sight. She kept on displaying and hooting as long as we were there, giving a good opportunity to see details of her display at close hand. This business of thrusting the chin forward, for example (the "chin" being the lower portion of the facial disk, including the white patches and the black patch that separates them), was especially striking. In this display, the black patch became more conspicuous, especially during hooting, for then that portion of the plumage flared out. I have noticed this in wild owls as well. It may well be that the black patch of feathers has a signal function in connection with aggression. It is of interest to note that the German name for this species – der bartkauz – means "bearded owl," in reference to the distinctive black patch or beard.

Grayl remained excited long after we had left the scene of this encounter, and I began to wonder how long she would remain in this mood. For the next two hours she stared fretfully out the back and side windows, giving everything that moved a hard look. Three hours after the incident her head was still a little larger than usual. By the time I turned her loose in her pen, she had dropped her display, but she still had an intense, suspicious air as she peered about. It was clear that she had carried the image of the wild owl all that time.

Grayl's strong reaction to a great gray owl or anything similar has, I'm pleased to note, some limit. When it comes to humans, her acceptance and perception knows no bounds. This bird knows and accepts people, people of all ages and sizes, all colours. She looks upon us with saintly benevolence, bestowing her tolerance with generous spirit. She even sees through disguises. On two occasions I've watched her closely when she was being approached by people wearing great gray owl costumes. This happened at Neepawa, where this is the town mascot, and at Winnipeg where a costumed figure of this species is the mascot of the Tourism Industry of Manitoba. Both costumes were delightfully rendered, artistic triumphs designed to imitate the great gray owl.

I was a little worried at Neepawa. The person wearing the owl costume there was a very tall man who approached Grayl from behind as she sat on her perch in the middle of a stage being videotaped. He was clearly hoping to get some reaction from her. As he neared her, he raised both his arms, the wings of the outfit. Just as I was ready to run forward to protest and to keep her from flying off her perch, she turned around and calmly looked him up and down as he flapped his wings, as if to say, "What a funny-looking outfit you're wearing." I needn't have worried. There simply was no reaction. In both cases, Grayl accepted each in turn for what she perceived them to be: people in disguise. There was no reaction, because she identi-fied the costumed figures as people. Not bad for an owl with a strong negative reaction to any real owl, dead or alive.

One cold January evening I found Grayl rigid with atten-tion in her pen, staring fixedly toward a distant woods to the south, visible because of the lack of leaves on our trees. I couldn't see anything to attract her attention, yet she refused to turn away, ignoring me when I prodded her. Finally I saw it, a great horned owl perched on the limb of an aspen, perhaps one hundred metres away. Not until the horned owl flew away did Grayl turn away from her vigil. A few weeks later, at 6:30 a.m. on January 23, 1988, I found her in a similar posture, "rigid, but not slim," intent on listening to what I took to be a calling great horned owl, a harsh "er-rark!," similar in rhythm to the begging call of an adult female great gray owl. Loud on this calm, dark morning, it caused a dog to bark, and then a large owl flew by, going fast to the north. Grayl turned and stared in that direction, upright and rigid long after it disappeared, looking as if she could still see it. Since great horned owls reside in this district, these birds may be the cause of her general watchfulness, especially in those hours when horned owls are on the move. Several times I have noticed Grayl behaving in just this way, listening and watching what I couldn't perceive.

At a mall, a mounted great horned owl in an exhibit drew a strong response from Grayl. Though the mount was old, faded and poorly done, it had all the characteristics she needed to identify it, even at a distance. I learned to be careful about approaching such things. On the other hand, since it didn't seem to leave a lasting effect, on several occasions I have demonstrated her display by deliberately showing her a mounted owl. One great horned owl mount elicited a striking display, an effective means of bringing a new aspect to a classroom. Grayl was hunched over, back feathers erected, tail spread wide and directed toward the mount, with one wing spread and held out. As I moved around her, she switched wings, enabling her to keep a wing presented without turning away, meanwhile she was snapping her bill, her eyes were large and round with small pupils – all the signs of extreme alarm. If I shoved the mount toward her, she reacted instantly, fanning her tail more widely, sharpening the display.

In one instance, as I approached Grayl with an old mounted great horned owl in a classroom, its head fell off. Naturally, the kids all laughed, but Grayl kept a steady eye on the decrepit mount until I put it away. It doesn't take much. Still, I was surprised the day she responded to a two-dimensional horned owl, a rather nicely done picture, that happened to be lying on a table in the gym where I had just finished putting Grayl on her perch. I didn't think it would work, but I held up the cardboard image and started walking toward her just to see if anything would happen. To my surprise, almost as soon as she noticed the outline of her nemesis, at 20 m or more distance, she responded with the usual big head, intense look and raised plumage display. I immediately withdrew it. Later I attempted to demonstrate this in front of the students, but there was much less response.

It needs to be said that one of the things we've learned from our studies of wild great gray owls is that their chief enemy is the great horned owl. Perhaps this is the reason great gray owls are especially wary late in the evening, that time of day when the more nocturnal great horned owls first become active. Both adults and young great gray owls have been killed and eaten by this slightly smaller, but heavier, predator. When grouse and hares are scarce, then great horned owls turn to other prey, taking what they can get, including our great grays. It should be no surprise, then, to find that Grayl is instinctively wary of that particular image.

One Eagle Too Many

A close encounter for the first time with a live golden eagle, a bird being exhibited at a mall in April 1987 by the Manitoba Wildlife Rehabilitation Organization, resulted in an alarming response by Grayl. It was an unintentional encounter, for I hadn't realized the eagle was present. As I passed by with Grayl on a glove, she suddenly went into extreme alarm, digging in with her claws, back feathers elevated, etc., while I hastened to take her to our booth. Then, upon seeing the eagle on its perch about 20 m away, she went into a more advanced display, dropping both wings down, tail fully spread, and head raised high with erect plumage. She held this posture stiffly for about eight minutes, relaxing only after I blocked her view of the eagle by shifting a TV set. Even then, she maintained a partial display for another eight minutes.

Four days later, when we were again at the mall, unfortunately the eagle was carried past us. The owl at once burst into the display. This time she seemed even more disturbed, for her breast was heaving, something I had not seen before. It was several minutes before she was back to normal.

At a later time, this behaviour was elicited with the use of a mounted golden eagle borrowed from Natural Resources. This gave us ample opportunity to observe and photograph Grayl's behaviour in greater detail, both with a still camera and later with a video camera. Since this display has not been

Intense response to golden eagle.

observed in wild great gray owls, it was of special interest to us. Repeatedly, as I moved the mounted eagle toward and then around Grayl who was perched atop an upright pole, we saw how she dropped one wing down at full length, directing it toward the eagle, then, as I moved around her, switching to the other wing. Both wings were held out to some extent, the one nearest the eagle being more fully extended. At first I had set the eagle on the ground about 20 m from Grayl, whereupon she showed considerable interest. When I carried it to her, she presented a spread wing to the mount, with tail fully fanned and pressed against the lowered wing. She repeatedly went from this to loud hooting, and then flying at the source of her annoyance, stopped only by the tether. On the ground, she went into a double-wings-up display, much like the typical defense posture of the long-eared owl.

Grayl's reaction to distant wild eagles has consisted mostly of watching them intently, following them until they move out of sight. On one occasion, however, she gave the erect alarm display to an eagle passing high over her pen (August 3, 1991, noon). She also, and this was new, hooted three times to the eagle which was several hundred metres overhead. She watched it with face tilted up until it was out of sight behind trees; only then did she relax.

A stronger reaction occurred on December 5, 1993, at Oak Hammock Marsh when Grayl happened to see a wild bald eagle at closer range than previously experienced. The eagle took flight from the ground about two hundred metres ahead of the car, whereupon Grayl bolted off her perch in the back of the car up onto the front seat between Rhonda O'Grady and me. It took a minute to sort things out, for Grayl, bristling and hooting with fury, was all over us, flapping wings and all. I couldn't decide whether she was trying to fly to attack the eagle or coming to us for protection.

Grayl seems to show a different response to various kinds of raptors, eagles eliciting a particularly strong reaction, but this is not well established. She vocalized again on

October 4, 1992, at noon, giving a single emphatic "hoo!" three times in two minutes to a red-tailed hawk soaring 200-300 m overhead. When I first turned to see why she had hooted, she was standing bolt upright, face turned up so far it was horizontal. She held this position for several minutes, inclining her face as the hawk moved on.

A Bigger Owl

Grayl's ability to make her head appear larger is often an impressive part of her agonistic display; by erecting the plumage of the head, it becomes the size of a soccer ball. She is defending herself, or strongly asserting herself, by making herself look as large as possible. This kind of display or behaviour is found in many, if not all, species of owls. It is agonistic behaviour, that is, it combines elements of both defense and attack.

In late December 1991, when Jim Duncan and I were out in the field looking for great gray owls to capture for banding, we found eight of them close together along the Maple Creek Road near Lac du Bonnet. There was a lot of social interaction going on that early morning; the owls were not so much out hunting for food, as watching each other. Several times we saw birds with the big heads characteristic of Grayl, responding to an opponent. Thanks to Grayl, we were better able to understand what was taking place that morning. Just as we can identify certain behaviour in Grayl because we have seen it in wild owls, so Grayl provides insights into what we've seen in the wild birds.

In another of Grayl's displays she makes herself look small instead of big. This curious and striking effect is achieved by assuming a tall, upright, narrow posture with wings pulled in tightly against the body and all the plumage compressed. In this display, the widest part of the bird is the head, an astonishing effect. And not the whole head either: it is the facial disk that is the widest part, this being the only area that can't be compressed. A little folding back of the disk

Menacing a new dog and a cat.

Response to strange dog.

takes place, but it is only slightly reduced in this pose. The tall, slim posture, a display observed in many species of owls, is generally known as the concealment posture. It is believed to help conceal a bird through its resemblance to an upright branch or stub. Of course, for full effect, this would have to be in a suitable situation. Recently, some authorities have viewed this display somewhat differently, preferring to call it the "erect alarm posture."

Fledgling great gray owls, and they leave the nest at three to four weeks of age, often assume the same tall, slim posture when we approach them. Their lack of adult plumage, however, makes their display much less striking. Perhaps adults, then, are assuming their own juvenile alarm posture.

I saw this display in Grayl before I ever saw it in a full-grown wild great gray owl, a suggestion that it may not be that common. Grayl rarely uses it. In fact, in nine years, I have seen her give the erect alarm display only about a dozen times. Although she is not afraid of dogs, she has given the display to dogs more often than to anything else. For example, at a Sportsman's Show, I noted: "On three occasions when a strange dog appeared nearby, she instantly went into the concealment display, upright and slim, so that she was very tall and slender, narrower than the facial disk, and with the right wing edge out and slightly forward...she held the display only briefly." It was as if the owl, exposed and restricted in movement to the perch and therefore vulnerable, didn't want to attract attention to herself, and so "withdrew" by assuming the display.

But even in the safe haven of her pen she has given the display to our own dog, with whom she is on familiar terms: "The owl sometimes responds to our dog running past her pen by assuming the tall, slim posture. She can instantly make herself slim. She relaxes just as quickly when the dog is past, then brings back the display when the dog returns." A week later, I noted: "She gives the display when our dog comes by and when she is in the right mood. She had been roosting quietly in the back of her pen, then she quickly draws her feathers

An elevated perch allows her to drop the entire wing in response to a mounted golden eagle.

tight, upright, the white-edged scapulars presenting a conspicuous scalloped pattern."

In several species of owls the outermost scapulars (the
feathers arising from the scapular or shoulder-blade region
and overlapping the base of the wing) are white or otherwise
conspicuously marked. As with other parts of the plumage,
this feature varies with the individuals. Although Grayl's
scapulars are not as white as in some birds I've seen, these
feathers still stand out markedly in this display. It seems likely
that this plumage feature offers additional disruptive col-
oration, adding to the camouflage effect achieved during the
erect alarm posture.

Also from her pen, "when a gray cat slinked past on its
usual route six metres away, the owl flew up onto a high perch
and went into a tall, slim posture, scapulars and wings pulled
in tightly. She watched the cat steadily, then broke off and fled
to the rear of her pen where she sat with hunched posture,
fluffed plumage, glowering, and gave an aggressive hoot."

One wing is dropped as far as it can go in response to a strange dog.

Well, cats are not always friendly, probably ranking as potential predators to an owl.

This next incident in her pen puzzles me. On May 3, 1987, I saw her in the "upright, elongated pose and then she went taller and leaned forward, without bending, to keep in view a young cottontail." I had been standing close by her, trying to figure out what it was that had caught her attention. The tiny rabbit was crouched down beside a brush-pile; it hardly seemed the sort of thing she should be so concerned about. Perhaps it was the first young one she'd ever seen.

A year later, when I saw her watching a great horned owl perched in a tree about a hundred metres from her pen, I was

Response to a new dog near the car.

struck by the fact that while Grayl was still and upright, she was decidedly not in the tall, slim concealment display. Two months later, however, "I found her in the erect posture, upright and slim, extreme concealment position, watching, or listening to, something to the north." Could she have been responding to a great horned owl?

Interpreting instinctive displays is fraught with difficulties. One can come upon a display part-way through, and one doesn't know the experience or the mood of the subject. The observations of Grayl's behaviour aided my perception of the erect alarm posture display the one time I saw it in a wild great gray owl. Herb Copland and I were watching an owl on April 1, 1989. It was a bird we had banded months before. Perched on a fairly high branch of an aspen tree close to a highway, it was in the usual relaxed posture of an alert hunting bird, moderately fluffed out and leaning forward slightly, face downward. Ten minutes later (we were having a cup of tea) it suddenly assumed the erect alarm posture. In this exaggerated tall, narrow pose it presented a very different image. The owl was looking straight back over its shoulder at first, then, slowly moving only its head, it turned its face around and up. I looked up at the sky and found what it was the bird was watching. An eagle, apparently an immature bald eagle, was flying about one hundred metres overhead and to the east of us, moving northwards. As the eagle drifted away, the owl resumed the relaxed attitude, leaning slightly forward.

My impression was that the owl, for whatever reason, wanted to stay on that particular branch, but in that exposed situation it reacted with the erect alarm posture to the sight of a large raptor passing overhead. It doesn't matter that eagles, especially bald eagles, rarely bother great gray owls. Presumably, this owl was responding not so much to the species of raptor, but rather to the raptor image. It's better to be safe than sorry!

In November 1990, at Lion's Place in downtown Winnipeg, Grayl responded to a raptor when it first appeared soaring overhead outside nearby high windows. She had been perched on her usual stand, watching people come and go, when suddenly she tilted her head upwards and stared fixedly. The raptor, a large buteo hawk, was soaring toward her and as it moved overhead she followed it, turning her head with a smooth, even motion.

I brought this to the attention of a number of people who were standing in front of the owl; they watched with interest, surprised by the intent look on the bird's face and by her obvious concern. I'd seen this before and, while intrigued, took it rather casually. But then something happened that startled me. When the raptor sailed overhead, beyond the windowframe and out of our sight, Grayl continued to track the bird, moving her head smoothly at just the right speed as if she could still see it and was following it. It was as if she could see through the roof, for the raptor had passed out of sight. At the time, I had no explanation for this highly unexpected behaviour.

Months later, it occurred to me that this event had special significance. The observation suggests that either the owl had retained an image of the moving raptor or else she had a grasp of the reality of the hawk's passage, an awareness of the hawk's position. This capacity for readily moving from what is seen to what is felt or thought suggests a level of consciousness beyond what is usually ascribed to birds.

This concentration of the owl upon a predator, and presumably, upon prey under food-seeking circumstances, may be involved in the unfortunate business of owls colliding with vehicles. There are now a number of observations of great gray owls and barred owls which were so intent on pursuing prey that they slammed into cars that had cut off their line of sight. The late Don Follen called this "focal concentration," a suggestion that birds will "see" the prey even when it's no longer in their sight.

After a day at a Winnipeg school (February 15, 1993), I drove out west of the city to show Grayl a snowy owl or two. It was late in the day, but we found one before it was time to turn back. Grayl showed enough of an interest in the owl to encourage me to take her back out the following afternoon. Though I'm not a photographer and my camera is not adequate for this kind of work, I had hopes of getting a snapshot of her response to a snowy owl.

In about an hour and a half we found six snowy owls. Two were perched high on power transmission towers, a tough angle for Grayl to see from her perch in the back of the car. I stopped by the first one and tried to direct her attention to the owl by repeatedly pointing up, but Grayl only scowled at my hand movements. The second owl, a little farther from the car and off to one side, eventually drew a little response from

Big show for a snowy owl.

Grayl. She tilted her head up steeply with out-thrust chin and stared intently; just as I reached for the camera, the owl flew away and Grayl dropped her pose.

The next two owls were both sitting on the snow, far out in the open, flat fields. Not much response. An owl on the cross-arm of a power pole about a quarter of a kilometre down the road ahead of us, however, had Grayl ducking her head and staring intently, back feathers slightly raised. I was getting frustrated looking for an owl, and then turning around in my seat so that I could watch Grayl and try to photograph her at an appropriate moment. I took a few pictures, but soon realized that I needed someone in the front seat to do the camera

"Not another farm dog?!" Note the big head.

work. Twice, passing cars frightened snowy owls off power poles just as I was getting in position.

My impression from this little workout was that Grayl reacted more strongly to the snowy owls that were darker, that is, the juvenile and female birds which, from a distance, sometimes appear almost black. The white males seemed to excite her less. Do the white ones look less like her mortal enemies, those dark great horned owls? Further observations might show something interesting, but there are too many factors involved for any strong conclusion.

We were heading home on a dirt road paralleled by a power line when we found the sixth owl, one I took to be an

Full response to an overly friendly farm dog.

adult female. This time, I turned the car around and drove slowly backwards to within 20 metres of the owl so that Grayl could get a good view through the large rear window – and she did! She erupted with fury and indignation, hooting loudly, back feathers straight up, wings thrusting down to the floor. I grabbed the camera but of course she had her back to me. Hoping the snowy owl would stay put, I jumped out, raised the hatch upright, exposing Grayl to an even clearer view, then kneeled on the bare black ground while trying to get Grayl framed for a picture. It was an anxious situation for all – Grayl huffed and puffed and stared malevolently while I scrambled about on my knees for a suitable angle. Anyone passing by would have been more than a little puzzled. It was -20°C, but the wind was low and the sun was bright; it was calm and peaceful. Still, when the snowy owl gracefully flew off to land in the field and Grayl settled down, I got back in the car in a hurry. Driving home with Grayl now quiet and attentive on her perch, I felt glad to be alive, happy in my situation.

Owl Bathing

She dips her head
and drinks
drinks again
peers over one shoulder
abruptly hops in
studies her reflection
looks around casually
lurches forward
onto her breast
with an embarrassed look
then, with a sigh, commits:
thrusts out her broad wings
thrashes violently —
for that moment she's
an ordinary bird
a robin, a sparrow...
in such quick immersion
they hold their fears
and bathe.

CHAPTER 7

On the Road

TRAVEL ACROSS AN INTERNATIONAL BORDER WITH A GREAT GRAY OWL sitting in the car can be interesting. I took Grayl through customs for the first time at South Junction, Manitoba, for a presentation nearby at Roseau, Minnesota. The Roseau Bog, as we came to call the large tamarack bogland just south of the border, has been one of our two main great gray owl study sites. Both U.S. and Canada customs officers there know us well and our Roseau visit had been well advertised locally. When I pulled up at the U.S. station, a customs officer came out, took one look, smiled broadly and waved us on through without a word.

When we drove to Duluth, we went through the port of Middlebro, just north of Warroad, Minnesota. Just to be on the safe side, I had phoned our contacts at South Junction and they made arrangements that ensured an easy passage. After I agreed to take Grayl to Minneapolis and La Crosse, Wisconsin, I made some official enquiries about travel to the U.S. It turned out that under the Convention on International Trade in Endangered Species (CITES), we were required to obtain an export permit. Correspondence between CITES personnel in Winnipeg, Ottawa and Minneapolis led to the provision of Temporary Export Permit No. CA-CW-TC-0043-90. In this document, there appears the following laconic description of Lady Grayl: "One Great Gray Owl with jesses plus an aluminum band on the left leg with the inscription 'Return to R. Nero', white bill, broken #6 tail feather." Even with this formidable document in hand, plus phone calls made in advance of our arrival, we encountered a delay at the U.S. customs at Noyes, Minnesota. A U.S. officer, a last minute substitute who had not been notified about us by headquarters, kept us worrying for a full thirty minutes while he pored through a large hand-book on rules governing transportation of endangered species. The delay didn't bother Grayl.

Sleeping with an Owl

We took Grayl on her first overnight trip in September 1989, driving to Duluth for a presentation that evening to the Minnesota Ornithologists' Union. Jim Duncan came along to help drive and manage things – a big help. I was worried about a lot of things in connection with this trip, but keeping Grayl overnight was my main concern. In the end, my contacts arranged to have the bird housed in a raptor flight pen in a friend's city backyard. It sounded not too bad.

Late that evening, after my talk, we carried a flashlight out to inspect the pen. It was small, dark and dirty, crammed with hawk-trapping equipment, and located way at the back of the yard – I had visions of raccoons getting in under the loose screen at the bottom – it wouldn't do! I hastily decided that it would be safer to keep Grayl in the car overnight, so we drove to the motel, parked, locked Grayl in the car, and went to our room.

Fifteen minutes later I had decided it was too risky: someone could break into the car, it was too small a space, better in the room with us, I suggested. Jim agreed and a few minutes later Grayl was on her perch, untethered, looking around the room with interest. We were a bit nervous about this arrangement, but I felt a lot better. Finally, we settled in and turned off the lights.

It wasn't a bad night – her first free flight around the room seemed awfully noisy for an owl, especially when she landed on the metal coat-racks, then flew onto the TV. We slept, aroused a few times by the wings of this eagle-sized bird flapping overhead. Once, early in the morning, I heard Jim give a shout and looked over to see Grayl perched on top of the covers, balancing on his foot. Long before it was time to get up, we were awake, enjoying the unusual treat of Grayl dropping onto first one bed and then the other, as if she were pouncing on a mouse. Jim told me that during the night the owl landed right beside his face. When he opened his eyes to see what had made a noise, she leaned forward and stared at him. He thought that she enjoyed this game, for a little later she came back and went through the same motions a second time. The best part was awakening to find that we – she and Jim and I – had survived our night together. Now we knew we could take the bird overnight.

That morning, up on Duluth's famous Hawk Ridge, Grayl was the centre of attention, attracting a crowd of birders delighting in the sight of a live great gray owl in the car. Despite Grayl being in the car and surrounded by admiring people, she was the first to pick out a distant osprey, her first, soaring over Lake Superior. The owl's sudden fixed stare with small pupils, chin thrust forward, tells us at once that she's found something significant in her world. That this object of importance should coincide with ours (at that time and place) is one more treat. She took all this in stride, sitting on her perch looking out the open hatch. I confidently left her in the charge of an admirer, then came running back when two mounted policemen came trotting around the corner to keep the road open. She'd not previously been so close to a horse, but this bothered her not at all. I was greatly relieved.

In May 1990, again with Jim Duncan providing assistance and encouragement, we headed off to Minneapolis and La Crosse, Wisconsin for an unprecedented four days and three nights away from home. With Grayl on hand, we drove down to Minneapolis in the afternoon, stayed overnight in a motel and gave a seminar to U.S. Forest staff at the University of Minnesota, then off we went to La Crosse.

The morning of the seminar we parked outside a restaurant to have breakfast. As always, I parked in a spot where we could keep an eye on Grayl from inside. A few minutes later a police car pulled up alongside and when the two officers peered into our car at the owl, I decided to go out to explain. I was surprised when one of the officers said: "That's a beautiful great gray owl!" It was the first live one he'd ever seen, but he'd enjoyed a TV program featuring great gray owls. We invited them to join us for breakfast and had a pleasant chat.

The process of getting the owl into a motel room varied. At Duluth, we had taken the bird in after dark, without asking anyone, but in the morning the young lady in charge – another owl-lover – was delighted with the arrangement. She recalled the event two and one-half years later, in 1991, when another owl-loving woman from Iowa drove 640 km to Duluth in hopes of seeing her first wild great gray owl. Beth Praeschaldt wrote to tell me that she and her son stayed in Duluth at a motel by the lakeshore, "the same one where 'a man and his wonderful owl' stayed once." My friends were rewarded by seeing an incredible nineteen great gray owls and one northern hawk owl on December 26 (my birthday!). Beth added: "We were ecstatic!! One lovely owl perched on a power pole 35-40 feet [10 metres] away, turning its head so the slight wind ruffled those delicate head feathers. I'll never blow on the feather over my bed, that you sent, but what I'll remember that!"

In La Crosse, Wisconsin, upon seeing a conspicuous "No pets allowed" sign, we sneaked the bird in the back way, but later invited staff into our room to meet Lady Grayl. No problem, she delighted everyone, and all agreed that she's not really a pet.

Each night on this long trek, I put out dead mice that I'd brought along, frozen and in a thermos bottle, but Grayl showed no interest in eating anything; she did drink more water than usual. A well-fed raptor clearly can go a few days without food, but it worried me.

Throughout the journey, Grayl showed a strong interest

in her surroundings. On the road, she never stopped scanning, turning about in all directions. Her ability to spot birds, especially large flying birds, delighted us. Crows always got a long look, but raptors, especially, held her attention, sometimes even after they were long behind us. Driving along the Mississippi River we frequently came across turkey vultures – it became a game to see how quickly we could spot them before she did. Despite her position on the perch in the back of the wagon, she was quick to see and react to these large soaring birds, giving each of them that beady-eyed look, that intense stare. Then, as we passed them, she'd swing her head around and watch them steadily until they were almost out of sight.

Occasionally, folks in cars or trucks behind us noticed our big bird and then drew up alongside us for a closer look. We were a little concerned about safety and drove cautiously under such circumstances. One event stands out: on the way home, driving on a Minnesota freeway, a red jeep sped along beside us. It took the driver some time to see what was happening as the black Labrador dog in the back of the open jeep leaned over the side, reacting to the owl that was giving her "big-and-ferocious" display, feathers all raised, wings extended and dropped, hooting to the dog! The black Lab wore a red ribbon, a nice touch. Both owl and dog held each other's attention as we sped along at 120 km/h. When the driver heard his dog barking he turned about, puzzled. Upon seeing the owl, he grinned widely and then proceeded to pace us for about 16 km, keeping alongside us until he had to turn off. We waved at each other before he turned away.

To Northern Manitoba

With the experience of the La Crosse trip behind us, a year later I found myself planning an even longer trip. When school teacher Olga Wesner from Cranberry Portage wrote to say that her kids were studying owls, and would I consider bringing the tame owl to that northern community, I was hesitant. Cranberry Portage is nearly 700 km north of Winnipeg, a long way to take an owl. However, at this time I had a paid assistant, and with the promise of support by Natural Resources staff in the north, it began to seem feasible. Great gray owls are fairly common in northern parts, or are seen more often than in the south. And yet, few people in the north have had a chance to see a great gray up close.

Eventually, we agreed to undertake a northern tour, with arrangements to visit schools in The Pas, Cranberry Portage, Flin Flon, Snow Lake, Grand Rapids and Easterville. It was a strenuous trip, but Grayl's ability for adjusting to and accepting new surroundings seems limitless. She spent the nights in two bunkhouses and two motels. From the car to overnight quarters, back to the car, into nine different schools, a mall and a trade show – all in six days in May 1991.

Consider how hard it is for us to adjust to new sleeping accommodations, though in most places everything is more

Rest stop, Rocky Lake, north of The Pas

or less familiar. Oh sure, when we first go into our room, we turn around a few times, flicking light-switches, drawing curtains, checking out the usual facilities. But for the owl, the only familiar object is her perch, always available and the central feature. Everything else is new, unfamiliar. Judging by her behaviour in motel rooms and bunkhouses, she adjusts more quickly than I do. At Cranberry Portage, I noted: "In the morning I draw the drapes back and open the screened window, whereupon she rushes to the windowsill, peers out and listens to a distant crow; she listens to the sounds of small birds, listens and looks to the woods."

Each time we take the owl into a new bedroom for the night, there is a period of exploration, first by me, then by her. I scan the room for things that might cause problems, disconnecting and removing ornate lamps from tables, removing or tying back unnecessary hangers that she could bang against,

Asleep – where else? – on a bunk, government bunkhouse.

bending down TV antennas, even removing nails from bunkhouse walls. The owl searches in her own way, measuring distances, then flying to perch on the back of a chair, on a table, on the TV set, on top of the coat-rack, on top of the curtain rods. Gradually she sorts out all possible perches, then rapidly takes control.

What does she feel, I wonder. I know that we can only interpret from what we see her doing. I try to imagine what it's like from her point of view, she who is so used to her familiar pen at home. What is it like, then, to have this feeling for the space and parts of a new situation? Her rapid acceptance suggests an orderly assessment and understanding of the limits, a flexible attitude, perhaps not much different from that of any wild owl settling onto a perch in new woods after a long journey.

That first night at The Pas, in a government bunkhouse at Grace Lake, Grayl kept us awake all night. When the owl wasn't hooting, she was landing with a crash on various items around the room, including the bedsprings of an empty bunk, a shelf,

Suppertime, Grace Lake.

a TV set, windowsill etc. The unexpected noise as She landed, clawing hard for purchase, was just as disturbing as her endless vocalizations. But consider the circumstances. We had driven all day long, starting out in a late cold spell, travelling on treacherous roads for one-third of the way to The Pas, in all about 600 km. It was pretty exciting for all of us, and I guess the owl was acting out her fantasies in her own way. My notes read: "She was surprisingly noisy, giving long, slow hoots which sound a little like a cellist drawing out a long note on a single tone, hooting with resonance and with control, halting, a demanding call that grabbed my attention in the dark. I cannot sleep. To say that she 'hoots' is inadequate. There is a wide range of expression in the way she hoots."

Phil Reader, The Pas, who showed us our first great gray owl nest.

While at The Pas, I took time to show Grayl to the man who showed me my first great gray owl nest in 1968. Talk about taking coals to Newcastle! We arrived at Phil Reader's rustic home on the shore of Reader Lake, only a short distance from where I'd first seen a great gray owl. Phil had learned from friends that we were touring schools in The Pas, so our visit was not a complete surprise. He grinned with delight as he bent down to look more closely at our bird. When I took her out of the car on the glove, he exclaimed: "Isn't that something!" We took the owl with us into the house and introduced her to his wife, Dorothy, just as one would a person. It was the first time I'd ever tried to drink tea and eat fresh bannock with one hand while holding the bird with the other.

Later, Phil and Grayl and I walked down to the edge of the lake. It had been more than 20 years since Phil and I had last seen each other, but there was no obvious gap. It was as if we'd never lost touch. Phil quoted Shakespeare while I held Grayl up to see the swans flying over the still-frozen lake. We talked quietly about mice and shrews, owls and hawks, the ways of woodland creatures. Phil, a former trapper, clearly had never lost his enthusiastic interest in the wild things he once so vigorously sought for fur. A curiosity about the ways of wildlife, that was our common bond. We hugged briefly on parting and Phil took one last look at "that great bird."

At a motel at Snow Lake, Lady Grayl was a little destructive. I had cleared away the usual potentially breakable or noisy items in the room, while Grayl sat on her familiar perch, then turned out the lights. It wasn't a bad night, but when I was getting ready to leave in the morning, I discovered that during her wanderings about the room she had shredded a bedspread on the second bed. Not good. I had noticed some reddish threads beneath her perch, had even picked them up and put them in the wastebasket. Then I turned around and discovered that she had torn two strips 2.5 cm wide and 25 cm long off the bedspread. What to do? I looked at the owl, but found no answer or guilt there; she just looked her usual self.

In her restlessness or out of boredom, she often picks at the carpeting wrapped about her perch, delighting school children when they see her biting and pulling away at the perch. And at our home, she has often pulled loose the short strands of yarn from the fringe of knitted pillows, but this was the first bedspread. In the end, I told the manager and his wife what had happened, expecting to have to pay something for the damage. Fortunately, I had invited the manager and his whole family in to meet the owl shortly after we had moved in the night before. When they saw the torn bedspread, they simply laughed at the notion of Grayl leaving her mark. "Don't worry about it," said the manager's wife, "that can easily be repaired."

Before we left Snow Lake, we visited wildlife artist Audrey Casey, whose realistic paintings of wolves and other northern animals may be found in homes across the country. I took Grayl into Audrey's house, and later we carried the owl outside for a photography session. At Audrey's request, I placed Grayl where she'd never before been, up on a branch in a live aspen

An open air break, Snow Lake.

tree, still safely tethered. My notes recall that sunny morning: "Suddenly I see Grayl in a new way... she delights in walking hand-over-hand along a slim limb, balancing with ease and grace; then she proceeds to snip off one twig after another, biting and dropping them with evident relish...she looks like a wild owl."

A Watchful Passenger

We can't ask Grayl, "What are you thinking?" as she watches the landscape rolling by as we speed down the highway, but we can at least try to understand what she is feeling. Hour after hour, something holds her attention. She is a tireless observer. Even I tire of looking at the landscape rushing past, especially when it's a monotonous one. But the owl has a seemingly tireless interest in the passing scene.

In trying to imagine what goes through her mind as we travel, what portion of the scene is registered, I consider what takes place with wild owls. A young owl emigrating hundreds of kilometres for the first time must be registering something. Some portion of the scenes of woods and lakes and rivers must be viewed and registered in some fashion. How else could it find its way back a year or two later, as Jim Duncan discovered? As we drive past meadows, forests, fields, towns, I am intrigued by this question – what does the owl see? She doesn't just sit and stare blindly at the passing scene, she looks at things, turns her head to look, holds it, then swings back again. She does this endlessly. First she fixes her attention on some aspect of the scene, then as the car speeds past, she swings her head back, following the point as it recedes, then turning back to yet another fix.

It took me some time before I realized that the owl was doing what we do! In a fast-moving car, it is almost impossible to look at things along the roadside, say, trees bordering the road, without shifting one's eyes as the trees recede. Try it, it's a strain! The act of trying to focus on the trees swinging past causes eyestrain. It can make me nauseous. What we tend to do is look at something, then follow it with our eyes as we move past and away from it. The owl, of course, can't shift her eyes – her eyes are immovable – hence she shifts her head every few seconds to focus on, and follow, a new object. In open country, her eyes fasten on more distant objects, a much easier situation to handle. It is just easier to look at more distant objects than things up close. Looking ahead or looking back, both are easier for man and owl than looking out the side.

The owl's scrutiny of the passing scene is more than merely staring blankly and letting the landscape sweep by. She sees things: for example, she watches birds with an admirable acuity, fixing on raptors as far away as they can be seen, dismissing gulls and crows and other large non-raptorial birds instantly. Her ability to pick out raptors in the midst of so many images delights us. Occasionally, I've noticed a distant buteo hawk circling low over fields at a time when Grayl's attention was on something else – then, at the last minute, she spies it!

I cheer for her ability, her adeptness in spotting her enemies. The owl has her eyes almost closed, dozing, when I spot a hawk, a red-tail, on the top of a power pole. I notice it because I look for hawks on top of poles, constantly searching as we go along. But will she see it as we whiz past? She does! The quick fix, as always, face tipped up, eyes alert, staring, and the head turn as we leave the hawk behind. In short, her search pattern must be like mine, we have this in common, we both look for the tell-tale form, added to the top of a post or pole, that is the perched raptor. Again, we watch together as another hawk – a northern harrier – floats lightly over a roadside pool, lifts over a fence and away. There is this pleasant sense of sharing, a mutual interest in hawks that keeps us watching for them. Just like any two people enjoying together the flight of a hawk, so the owl and I are like companions, reacting together to the same thing. It makes me feel close to her.

One would think that an owl confined to a car would feel insecure if approached by a strange dog. On occasion, her behaviour suggests otherwise. One morning at Flin Flon, parked at a lakeside cafe to have breakfast, I observed her response to both a dog and a cat. The cat, a young black and white one, strolled past the car, evidently not noticing the ferocious display its presence aroused in the owl. Grayl was on top of her stump-perch, both wings spread and cocked upright, owing to the short distance available below the perch. Her display looked much like the defensive display of the long-eared owl. By and large, strange cats seem to elicit a greater response than do dogs. A few minutes later, after parking the car in a place where we could better keep an eye on it, a dog came by. The large German shepherd started toward the car when it first noticed the owl on her perch, then backed off when the bird ruffled her plumage and, judging by her behaviour, also hooted vigorously. This went on for several minutes, causing my companion to wonder if it wasn't stressing the owl too much. But, I explained, one could see that the owl was dominating the dog

Fierce look to a new dog and cat.

– an interesting situation. In the end, although the owl kept a wary eye on the dog, it was clear that the dog was being kept at bay by the bird. Every now and then the dog circled the car, always keeping at a respectful distance and with its eyes averted, to which the owl responded with only moderate concern. Thus, the submissive behaviour of the dog had meaning for the bird.

To Thompson and Beyond

In May 1992, I undertook an even more arduous tour, going by myself even farther north to Thompson and Gillam. The latter town is at the end of the road on the Lower Nelson River, about 1000 km from Winnipeg. The trip appealed to me because our youngest son, Brook, and his family were living in Gillam and I had promised him that some day I would bring the owl up. They were planning to move away from there at the end of summer, so this was my last chance to make good on my promise. On top of that, a cheerful, enthusiastic grade-three teacher at Thompson, Jodi Stepaniuk, undertook to make many of the necessary arrangements, booking me into six schools in Thompson and one in Gillam, and fixing an itinerary.

On the way to Thompson, I stopped a few times, always getting a lot of questions about the big owl in the car, for she is not easily overlooked. Just south of Ponton, about two-thirds of the way to Thompson, I took time to make a quick search for prehistoric artifacts on some bare sand ridges close to the highway. As I hurried from one open patch to another, I could see Grayl in the locked car. To my delight, there were a few flint flakes, a sure sign of early occupation; a few minutes later I found a flint end-scraper, a distinctive tool for cleaning animal skins in preparation for making clothing. What a great way to begin my northern owl tour! I placed the shiny scraper on the dashboard and kept looking at it all the way to Thompson. On the return trip, six days later, I checked five other eroded sites in the same general area, always keeping the car in sight. I found more flakes, two more scrapers, and fresh tracks of moose, sandhill cranes, a wolf and a cougar. Cougars aren't that common here, so I took some time to make notes on the size of the tracks and the length of stride. Meanwhile, Grayl sat patiently on her perch in the car.

The road north from Thompson to Gillam is a long rough stretch of gravel, so when Brook offered to drive down to pick us up, I accepted. The owl had the same perch in the back of my son's truck, only different windows and a slightly different arrangement of things around her. For the length of that trip, over new terrain for both the owl and myself, she never stopped looking. Four hours of black spruce forest, lakes and streams, almost monotonous at times, but the owl watched with untiring attentiveness as if she were really interested, looking first to one side, then to the other, then looking back over her shoulder at the receding scene. I thought of the wild owls flying over and through this landscape, for several of our radio-marked birds had found their way to Gillam and beyond.

"I know snow, but what's Labrador tea?"

I wondered whether Grayl's genes supplied her, somehow, with some sense of recognition of this rolling, unfolding vista. We drove from 8:00 p.m. to past 12:00 p.m., yet even in the dark this seemingly indefatigable bird continued to scan the passing scene.

We arrived in Gillam after midnight, expecting to lodge the owl and myself in a government bunkhouse. It proved to be inadequate for our needs, so we went to my son's house. By nailing up some blankets and a tarp, we were able to convert the basement rooms to satisfy my requirements for safe housing for Grayl. In the morning, I was greatly relieved to see that she had sustained no accident during the night. When Brook's four-year old son Joshua awoke, he was pleased to find his "grandpa-owl" and the owl at his house. We had a good visit and everyone came to see the presentation at the Gillam school; Grayl, as always, was a great success. The following morning, on the way back to Thompson, we drove to Sundance, a small temporary community on the Nelson River. It had snowed that morning, converting the sparse boreal forest along the high bank of that wide river to a clean, sparkling-white fairyland. Grayl viewed it all in her usual calm manner, but she seemed pleased to walk in the snow.

Perhaps the best example yet of this bird's keen eyesight took place on the way back from Thompson. I had pulled into a service station just off the highway at St. Martin on May 17. In a few minutes four people had gathered behind my vehicle, looking at the owl through the rear hatch window, while the owl solemnly stared back. Suddenly, the owl's head tipped up and her pupils contracted in an intense locked stare...she froze, like a dog on point. "Hawk overhead" I guessed out loud, and searched the empty sky. But then an older native man, obviously one with good eyesight, pointed to a bird high above. It took me a moment to spot it, but there it was, an eagle circling, soaring far above us. Grayl stayed fixed on the bird, tilting her face up and up as the eagle gradually moved over and past us, ignoring the people watching her, until her face was nearly horizontal. Shortly after the eagle passed out of her sight, she relaxed and returned to looking at her visitors.

Coming Home

For the past hour she has dozed, eyes at times nearly closed, mostly motionless on her perch. We're on the home stretch, sailing down the highway, Winnipeg not far ahead. It's snowing again, a light flurry, wet on the windshield on this late April evening. We're returning, the owl and I, from three days in Dauphin where we toured schools. It is a relief for me to have the tours over, anxieties behind me for the moment. I don't know how the owl feels, but she seems tired, and she ought to be after entertaining several hundred people, and spending two nights in another government bunkhouse.

Then, as we near the Perimeter Highway, she becomes alert, sits straighter, eyes open again, watching ahead. By the time we're in the city, only a few miles from home, I'm convinced that she's aware that we're coming home. She's fully alert and watchful as we turn onto our street and then pull into the driveway. It's good to be back, and I'm pleased with the sight of the familiar yard, lawn greening slightly, a light snow still falling. We're back. I'm in the house only long enough to say hello, and to pick up the four mice Ruth has carefully set out on the kitchen counter. I put them in my coat pocket, then hasten to take the owl out of the car to return her to her pen. She's all eyes, climbs right up onto my gloved hand, and flaps vigorously when I hold her up high for my usual half-run, owl aloft, to the pen. She's excited, as always upon returning to her home – the sight of the spruce trees, pools of meltwater, and pen seem to arouse her.

Released into her pen, as always flying right up onto her high perch, she sits up high. It's HER place, and she seems to savour it. I stand by, striving to see things from her perspective, and succeed a little, I think. A robin calls, loud, clear notes; geese call overhead in the darkening mist; there is a muted roar of nearby traffic; a drake mallard quacks severely from low in the sky. It is lovely. The owl then turns about, drops onto the ground, steps lightly, skirts raised, walks quickly to a mound of snow, ecstatically throws herself upon it – there's no other way to describe it – thrusting her breast or belly down onto the snow, again and again. Oh, she's home alright. I've never seen her so enthusiastic about her pen, have never before seen her crouch down on the snow – it's almost as if she felt some urge to incubate, or brood something cold and white. Or is she snow-bathing, as ravens do? Now she hops up onto her stump, pecks at the surface, stares out through the trees. I stand beside her but she ignores me. Up she flies onto a high perch again, then a fast flight to the rear of the pen, and a quick return, all repeated twice more, before she slows down.

She ignores me, though she sees me, when I first hold out a mouse, then place them one by one in a row on her feeding shelf. I have to force myself to stop watching her – this

All of us feeling fall.

is intriguing! Then I turn and look at our house, and there's Ruth in the window, watching me, thinking her secret thoughts about her husband and the owl. It is a warm and loving moment. My life is full and good. I walk back to the house, retracing my steps in the thin layer of wet snow.

The Owl's Gift

In the dark rainy night
I consult with this oracle
reaching through soft feathers
to feel her warm throat
thinking as I do that
the fabric of her being
is mere thin skin stretched
over braced bones and flesh
a fragile assemblage
to so command our attention.
So then where's the spirit of
this comforting creature that
ceaselessly charms us all?
It must be in her mind
(do birds have minds?)
it's in her attitude, the way
she trusts us and accepts us;
she comes from her owl-being
to meet us in her time
gravely allowing us a
glimpse of her world
a gift of tender tolerance
we do well to honour.

Bibliography

Bouchart, M.L. 1991. Great gray owl habitat use in southeastern Manitoba and the effects of forest resource management. M.N.R.M. Practicum thesis, Nat. Res. Inst., Univ. Man., Winnipeg. 92pp.

Bull, E.L., and J.R. Duncan. 1993. Great gray owl (Strix nebulosa). In: The Birds of North America, No. 41 (A. Poole and F. Gill, Eds.). The Academy of Natural Sciences, Philadelphia; The American Ornithologists' Union, Washington, D.C.

Collins, K.M. 1980. Aspects of the biology of the great gray owl. M.S. thesis, Univ. Man., Winnipeg. 219pp.

Duncan, J.R. 1987. Movement strategies, mortality, and behavior of radio-marked great gray owls in southeastern Manitoba and northern Minnesota. In: Nero et al., 1987.

Duncan, J.R. 1992. Influence of prey abundance and snow cover on great gray owl breeding dispersal. Ph.D. thesis, Univ. Man., Winnipeg. 127pp.

Farner, D.S., and J.R. King, Eds. 1972. Avian Biology, Vol. 2. Academic Press, New York, 586pp.

Follen, D.G., Sr. 1986. Barred owl: a demonstration of focal concentration. Passenger Pigeon 48: 73.

Goulden, R. 1987. Meeting the outdoor ethics challenge in Canada. In: Proceedings of the International Conference on Outdoor Ethics. Lake Ozark, Missouri.

Hamerstrom, F. 1970. An Eagle to the Sky. Iowa State University Press, Ames. 143pp.

Hamerstrom, F. 1986. Harrier: Hawk of the Marshes. Smithsonian Institution Press, Washington, D.C. 171pp.

Heinrich, B. 1987. One Man's Owl. Princeton Univ. Press, New Jersey. 224pp.

Heinrich, B. 1989. Ravens in Winter. Summit Books, New York. 379pp.

Johnsgard, P.A. 1988. North American Owls: Biology and Natural History. Smithsonian Institution Press, Washington, D.C. 295pp.

Lawrence, L. de K. 1976. Mar: A Glimpse into the Natural Life of a Bird. Clarke, Irwin & Co. Ltd. Reprinted by Natural Heritage/Natural History Inc., Toronto, 1986.

Loch, S.L. 1985. Manitoba great gray owl project, progress report, April 1, 1984 - August 1, 1985. Mimeo. Man. Wildlife Branch Files.

Mackrill, E. 1986. Scops owl sunbathing. British Birds 79: 296-97.

McKeever, L. 1986. A Dowry of Owls. Lester & Orpen Dennys Ltd., Toronto. 208pp.

Nero, R.W. 1980. The Great Gray Owl, Phantom of the Northern Forest. Smithsonian Institution Press, Washington, D.C. 167pp.

_____ 1985a. "Gray'l" – fund-raiser extraordinaire. Manitoba Naturalists Society Bull. 8 (3): 4-6.

_____ 1985b. Gray'l attracts lots of attention. Manitoba Naturalists Society Bull. 8 (10):6.

_____ 1989. The story of "Gray'l." The Manitoba Outdoorsman. Fall 1989: 17.

_____ 1990. Woman by the Shore, and Other Poems. Natural Heritage/Natural History Inc., Toronto. 51pp.

_____ 1991. Focal concentration: a possible cause of mortality in the great gray owl. Blue Jay 49: 28-30.

_____ 1993. The Mulch Pile, and Other Poems. Natural Heritage/Natural History Inc., Toronto. 95pp.

Nero, R.W., R.J. Clark, R.J. Knapton, and R.H. Hamre. 1987. Biology and Conservation of Northern Forest Owls: Symposium Proceedings. USDA Forest Service, Gen. Tech. Report RM-142. 309pp.

Norberg, R.Å. 1987. Evolution, structure, and ecology of northern forest owls. In: Nero et al. 1987.

Quinton, M.S. 1988. Ghost of the Forest, the Great Gray Owl. Northland Press, Flagstaff, Arizona. 97pp.

Scriven, R. 1984. A note on albinism in the great gray owl. Blue Jay 42: 173-74.

Servos, M.C. 1987. Summer habitat use by great gray owls in southeastern Manitoba. In: Nero et al., 1987.

Toops, C. 1990. The Enchanting Owl. Voyageur Press, Stillwater, Minn. 128pp.

Voous, K.H. 1988. Owls of the Northern Hemisphere. MIT Press. Cambridge, Mass. 320pp..

"Everybody wants my picture."

Photography Credits

Front Cover:	Brook A. Nero
Back Cover:	George Hunka, Canadian Publishers
Page 14	Norman R. Lightfoot
Pages 21, 22, 24, 27	Scriven family
Page 29	Dennis Fast
Page 35	James O'Connor
Page 37 (top)	Robert Charach
Page 37 (bottom)	James R. Duncan
Page 39	Ray Cormier
Page 40	Cole family
Page 41	Ted Muir
Pages 43, 46	Don Campbell
Pages 55, 61, 62, 69	Author
Page 77	Dave Johnson, Winnipeg Free Press
Page 88	Wanda McConnell, Canadian Publishers
Page 94	Catherine Diduck
Page 96	Carol Ball
Pages 114, 117, 118, 120	Jackie Atkinson
Page 132	Author
Page 134	Astral Photo
Page 139	Robert R. Taylor
Page 142	Author
Page 144	Robert R. Taylor
Pages 145, 146, 149, 150, 151,	Author
Pages 159, 160, 161, 162, 164	Corinna Jasienczyk
Page 167	Author
Page 169	Brook A. Nero
Pages 172, 176	Ray Cormier

Printed in the USA
CPSIA information can be obtained
at www.ICGtesting.com
JSHW012032140824
68134JS00033B/3020

9 780920 474945